中國的菜園

中國的菜園

THE CHINESE KITCHEN GARDEN

growing techniques
and family recipes
from a classic cuisine

WENDY KIANG-SPRAY
with photography by Sarah Culver

TIMBER PRESS
PORTLAND, OREGON

Frontispiece: Green radishes are easy to grow and good for the garden. They are packed with nutrition and taste even better after a frost when they earn the nickname "radish sweeter than pear."

The Haseltine Building
133 S.W. Second Avenue, Suite 450
Portland, Oregon 97204-3527
timberpress.com

Printed in China
Text and cover design by Patrick Barber

Library of Congress Cataloging-in-Publication Data

Names: Kiang-Spray, Wendy, author.
Title: The Chinese kitchen garden: growing techniques and
    family recipes from a classic cuisine / Wendy Kiang-Spray.
Description: Portland, Oregon: Timber Press, Inc., 2017. |
    Includes bibliographical references and index.
Identifiers: LCCN 2016009572 | ISBN 9781604696776 (pbk.)
Subjects: LCSH: Vegetables, Chinese. | Kitchen gardens.
Classification: LCC SB351.C54 K53 2016 | DDC 635—dc23 LC
    record available at https://lccn.loc.gov/2016009572

A catalog record for this book is also available
from the British Library.

For my parents, my maternal grandfather and grandmother, and especially for Wan Lan Wong.

Wan Lan Wong, a grandmother I did not know but whose spirit inspired and runs through this book.

FALL 137

秋
天

WINTER 207

冬
天

preface

Thank you. I am truly thrilled and humbled that you are reading this book. This is not only because I hope you will find it useful as you grow the vegetables that my family has known for generations, but because among the smooth sweet potato leaves, the tangled luffa gourd vines, and the giant winter melons is my family's story. While I personally have work to do in tracing my history back beyond the fuzzy tales I've learned about my grandparents, I know that simple chores in my garden or weekend dinners with my parents are all made up of their cumulative experiences, at the same time tumultuous and wonderful. To make sense of my own story, I had to know my parents' stories.

my father's story

When my father was a boy, he planted a Chinese date tree in his small rural village in Shandong, China. He cared for this tree for many years until it bore abundant fruit. With the arrival of communism, his family was systematically stripped of its money and belongings. My father, his brother, and his mother were thrown out of their large home because it was deemed a better fit for village elders representing the Communist Party. Later, even the fruit from his tree would be considered community property. By the late 1950s, when my father was about thirteen years old, he was angry and destitute, and his family had resorted to living in an abandoned house believed to be haunted. He decided that there was one thing he *could* control: no one would take claim over the tree he himself cultivated. And so one evening, he chopped it down in quiet protest. When the village elders heard about this act of defiance, he was accused of destroying state property and publicly flogged to set an example for the rest of the villagers.

My father's garden story began as one shaped by protest and survival. Politics and community pressure made life difficult for him and his family, but their spirit and perseverance would not be broken. Farming and growing food came to play a huge role in their lives. They ate only what they grew or could barter for.

Bitter melon vines climb up and over a bamboo arbor. By mid-summer, fruits are ready for picking.

In the bleak winter months, their diets consisted of Napa cabbage and radishes brought up from pits in the ground that served as cold storage. Cooking oil was scarce, so the stir-fries that are commonplace in Chinese cuisine today were a rare treat. Occasionally, they would mix vegetables with a small amount of shrimp paste or another fermented food to add flavor and break the monotony of their daily meals. Along with this, they would have some bread made of corn, which they grew each summer, dried, and ground themselves. And yet my father insists that these meals were delicious—a reflection of both their austere living conditions as well as their optimism and determination to triumph over the situation.

In his mid-twenties, my father managed to reach Hong Kong, learned to speak Cantonese, and adopted a new culture. He discovered that foods like bitter melon, which he was accustomed to growing for its sweet and goopy mature pulp, could be eaten another way. In Hong Kong restaurants, the bumpy green flesh was cut into chunks, stir-fried, and enjoyed for its refreshingly bitter taste. He also learned how to be a businessman, and in 1974—the year I was born—he moved with his wife, my mother, to the United States, where he started a business importing Chinese art and antiques.

Eventually my parents bought a home, and the land that came with it rekindled my father's desire to grow food. Although the 1980s were good to my parents and they no longer had to grow food to survive, old habits die hard. I can imagine my father as a young man, standing in the backyard, studying the sun, purchasing his first American spade, and turning over the soil as any gardener would be driven to do.

my mother's story

My mother is the second eldest of seven children: one boy, the rest girls. Their father, a stern man who worked hard under the burden of having so many mouths to feed, died when the children were still young. This meant that the older children had to spend much of their time caring for their younger siblings, while my grandmother sought work every day. My mom stopped attending school at a young age and instead began cleaning, caretaking, and cooking for their family of eight. She has always had a knack for domestic responsibilities. She takes pride in her cooking and uses it to express her love for her family.

My mom married my father and then moved with him to the United States when she was about 22 years old. Although they had been used to hunger and scarcity, through a combination of hard work and luck, they were able to live the American dream. Today, they enjoy a beautiful home landscape to behold daily and have an abundance of food. Ironically, on summer evenings when my father walks into the kitchen with baskets of vegetables, my mom fusses and complains about him growing too much—because then it's up to *her* to figure out how to prepare or preserve all those vegetables.

My parents are both true gourmets and skilled home cooks. My mom makes incredible stir-fries, soups, and stews, and is an expert at traditional food preservation. My father is a master at crafting handmade noodles, dumplings, steamed buns, and breads. These are all foods that Chinese people savor but few can create. We have always been a family of culinary connoisseurs. My sister and I grew up eating unfamiliar and delicious dishes in the best Chinese restaurants, and then enjoying even better versions of the meal at home when my parents recreated the food we tasted the previous weekend (or that they saw in a Chinese movie, or remembered from a joint they ate at in Hong Kong decades ago). My father has even recreated a dumpling filling made from an heirloom Chinese squash he last tasted in his village in China in the 1960s.

As children, my sister and I could mark time with the familiar sound of my

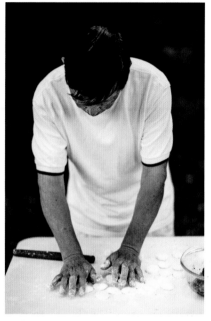

Homegrown and home-cooked leafy green vegetables have a place year round on the dinner table.

My father, preparing to make his highly coveted dumplings.

mom cooking in the kitchen. First the chopping, then the hum of the kitchen range fan, then the hiss of garlic and greens dropping into a hot wok. The steel wok spatula clanged as she cooked, and then scrape, scrape, scrape as the stir-fry was transferred onto the serving plate. Finally, the fan would turn off and the sudden quiet meant dinner was ready.

my story

My own garden story didn't begin until I was an adult. When my older daughter was seven years old, she suddenly said, "Hey, Mom, let's have a garden!" and my obsession with gardening began.

Though he has mellowed with age, my father has always disapproved of my interests. A life of hardships, the lack of a father figure as a role model, and Chinese cultural norms meant that my father never outwardly expressed pride in me and would often be dismissive. His stubborn temperament, like mine, meant that a disagreement on any innocuous topic—such as whether my children's jackets were warm enough—could promptly escalate to a screaming match. Call me a glutton for punishment, but despite this, I have always consciously or subconsciously sought to gain his approval.

My father's immense vegetable garden dwarfs my entire backyard. Ducks swim contentedly around his immaculate 6-acre pond edged with lotuses and water lilies. Many evenings my father can be found fishing from the pier and deck he built himself. As an experienced gardener, he probably knew full well that my garden would offer challenges. A large maple tree casts shade over half my backyard. The virgin soil was less than ideal. The garden would be tiny. What did he think of my exciting new gardening idea? "No air! No sun! You can't grow anything!" So what did I do? Set out to prove him wrong. Just as we're both stubborn, we're also both ambitious and determined.

I tapped into the wealth of information on the Internet and studied into the wee hours of the night. I took notes, printed photos, joined gardening forums, and asked hundreds of questions. In the mornings, the thought of seed and plant catalogs sitting on the kitchen table got me out of bed early. I learned we were in hardiness zone 6, and then learned what that actually meant. I became fluent in botanical Latin, and memorized the soil, light, and moisture requirements for almost everything in Kingdom Plantae.

Armed with this knowledge, I drew up a plan, built some beds, and bought some seeds. It is not impossible to begin gardening at this later stage in life—you just have to learn quickly from your mistakes. It didn't take long for me to learn that you don't support tomatoes with pencil-thin bamboo stakes. Or that dumping clay soil in a corner of the yard doesn't make a compost pile, but simply makes a pile of clay soil in the corner of the yard.

I delved full force into my garden, beginning with a tiny wooden raised bed that has changed in shape and gotten a little bigger each year. Soon thereafter, I found an interest in perennials and completed an overhaul of my front yard. After that, I feverishly planned and then tackled a DIY stone retaining wall and landscaping job in my backyard. I was so busy that I barely felt the need to share what I was doing with anyone, especially with my father.

One year, I grew 'Cherokee Purple' tomatoes for the first time. Because my father's a big tomato grower, I thought it would be a shame if he didn't at least get to taste the delicious results and know about the different colors, shapes, sizes, and tastes that are characteristic of heirloom tomatoes. I assumed that my tomato wouldn't live up to his expectations, so I was shocked when he not only liked the taste, but was interested in obtaining some seed. The next year, he planted twenty 'Cherokee Purple' tomatoes in his garden and only a few of his usual beefsteaks. He also asked me to order some beet seeds for him—this from a man typically too proud and independent to ask his daughter for anything.

My father rarely expresses his feelings. However, despite his initial disparaging remarks, I know in no uncertain terms how he feels about my gardening. One day, as I was at my parents' house for dinner, I was flipping through some albums containing photos my father had taken. There, in the middle of all the other haphazardly inserted photos of his beautiful property, pond, and fruit trees, were photos he had secretly taken of my own humble first-year garden.

our family story

When my father realized I was serious about gardening, he began to teach me more about growing vegetables in earnest. While my sister and I grew up in the garden, it had primarily been our father's hobby. And while we occasionally asked for our own plots, he must have been too much of a control freak, and perhaps had too little patience for teaching young children, because our gardens ended up right back in his hands just as soon as we planted our first seeds. Of course, it's quite possible that riding bikes with neighborhood friends tore us away from tending said gardens.

One late spring evening, my kids played outside while my father and I sat on the driveway preparing a giant basket of bamboo shoots he'd just harvested. To break the silence, I asked him what kinds of vegetables he grew in China and the stories began to surface. As children, my sister and I liked to eavesdrop on conversations between our father and uncle, hearing bits and pieces of unpleasant stories such as the one about the first morning after they slept in the haunted, abandoned house. They awakened to find a crowd of nosy villagers gathered outside the front door, anxious to learn if they were still alive. We were young and wanted to know more, but every time we asked for more details, my mother or my uncle would hush us up. We grew up knowing our father's childhood was rough and we learned never to ask about certain topics.

By telling me the story of the Napa cabbage pits, my father painted a clear and vivid picture of the life he lived, and I was able to ask where the garden was located, what the daily chores were, and what their house, in a village long demolished, looked like. As time went on, I even learned a tiny bit about his mother, who died before I could know her. Like other villagers, my father would go to the market to sell surplus crops, kindling he'd collected, or silk from the silkworms he'd raised. At the same market, my grandmother sold hand-sewn beautiful shoes, cut from the embroidered silk fabric of the expensive ornate dresses, now useless, that she had owned before the Communist takeover. I learned what a practical, skilled, and formidable woman she had been, and I like to think that my ability to work with my hands comes from her. Asking my

With my sister, Lisa.

father about the vegetables he grew, and the way he farmed, gives me insight into a world I yearn to know but that would otherwise be far too painful to talk about openly.

For an Asian American child growing up in the 1970s and 80s, assimilation was the expectation. As a member of the first generation to be born in the United States, I don't have a Chinese name. English was my first language, and I never brought Chinese food in my school lunch for fear of looking weird. Trapped between two cultures, like many of my generation, I spent a lot of time during my youth wanting to keep my Chinese side under wraps.

As an adult, and especially as an adult whose children are biracial, I'm concerned that my Chinese ancestry will eventually be lost through future generations. Fortunately, my children identify as being Chinese and are fully proud of and immersed in Chinese culture. For them, and for me, I want to know as much as I can, remember as much as I can, and learn as much as I can about a life from another time on the other side of the world. My father's garden stories and my mother's food stories help me to understand my own identity. Recording these stories is crucial to keeping our culture, ethnicity, and legacy alive.

When my sister learned this book would become a reality, she said, "You're going to be able to tell our story." This is how I view this book. I hope it will be a good starting point for readers to learn how to grow and use the vegetables I have included. But I also hope readers will be able to learn more about Chinese culture through my explanations of how to enjoy these vegetables. The story I tell is a personal one, like my sister said, and I thank you for indulging us by reading this book.

about this book

The vegetables I chose for this book are all connected by their strong place in the foodways of China. Chinese civilization has a long history, and over the millennia trade moved these vegetables back and forth between neighboring countries. That's why eggplant (*Solanum melongena*) may be known as either Japanese or Chinese eggplant. Regardless of where it originated, every vegetable in this book is either native to China, commonly thought of as Chinese, or plays a solid role in the culinary world of China.

The beginning of each vegetable profile includes the plant's common name, Chinese transliterations, pronunciations in Mandarin and Cantonese, and botanical name. With a country as large as China, and a reach into neighboring and faraway countries, much variation is to be expected. For example, my father grew up speaking Mandarin, as do most people in Northern China. When he moved to Hong Kong, he learned Cantonese, the common language of people in the Canton and Hong Kong regions. While I grew up hearing both languages, particularly when my father had conversations with my uncle in Mandarin, Cantonese is the first language of most of my family members and is the language my parents speak. It is also the language in which my mother speaks to me and is the language I think in. Keep in mind that a vegetable's common name may be its Chinese name, such as bok choy, or may be derived from another language, like tatsoi, which comes from its Japanese name. Or, it may simply be a description, such as Chinese cucumber. A vegetable's name may also be written using its Chinese characters. All these language variations can make for a confusing experience when shopping for seeds, which is why I have provided several variations for the names of each vegetable. Throughout this book, I have

My sister, Lisa, and me, our families, and our parents.

used the Pinyin system of romanization, which presents a few quirks for speakers unfamiliar with Mandarin. Some of the most common are the following:

C is pronounced like the *ts* in ha*ts*.
H is pronounced like the *ch* in Scottish lo*ch*.
Q is pronounced somewhat like the *ch* is *ch*est.
X is pronounced somewhat like the *sh* in *sh*irt.
Z is pronounced like the *ds* in su*ds*.
Zh is pronounced like the *dg* in ju*dg*e.

You will find information about how to successfully grow each vegetable in its profile. Some of the vegetables in this book, such as eggplant and cilantro, are relatively well known and easy to grow in any garden. Others, such as taro root or lotus, may be more obscure or require special growing conditions. The vegetables in this book are organized by the season during which that vegetable is at its prime for harvesting. Take note that vegetables such as lotus root require a long growing period. Vegetables such as garlic chives are fantastic in spring or fall, but especially when started a couple seasons prior. I suggest reading the entire entry to be sure the vegetable is a good match for your climate and garden conditions, and also to plan ahead, if necessary, before getting started.

China is a vast country, with climates and conditions that range from arctic to tropical, but when I refer to Chinese gardens, I mean the culturally specific preferences of gardeners in China. Of course, Chinese gardeners make use of a range of practices from conventional (the use of synthetic fertilizers and pesticides) to fully organic. In my garden, I strive to grow food using organic methods, so these are the only recommendations I make in this book.

Following the growing information, I share how to prepare and use each vegetable in the kitchen. I also indicate whether it will work as an alternative to a vegetable already in your repertoire. The recipes represent a range of foods that I love and that I think you should experience. While the measurements and cooking times will give you a starting point for any dish you have not cooked before, or maybe not even tasted, I hope you will flavor, season, and vary your dishes however you see fit. Some recipes, like braised bamboo shoots and pork belly, are more traditional and time intensive, while others, such as the bok choy stir-fry, are excellent for quick weeknight preparations. I share recipes for congee and other lesser-known comfort foods, as well as recipes that will surely impress your friends, like one often-requested variation of my father's dumplings. No matter how simple or involved, you can be certain that all recipes are delicious and authentically Chinese.

SPRING

春
天

Spring has a quality that is distinct from other times of the year. The air is filled with a sweet earthiness, cool rains are refreshing, morning mists linger, and warm days breathe life into new foliage and budding blossoms. In our family, and perhaps in yours too, spring drives us outside. My husband lazes under a tree with a new book picked out from his to-read stack. My mom walks around the large circular stand of bamboo wondering when shoots will emerge, signaling long afternoons of harvesting, preparing, and transforming the tender shoots into dishes we look forward to every year. My younger child, Lyric, flits here and there ›

Spring brings the most tender first flush of garlic chives.

beckoning everyone to play one of her springtime games, usually involving throwing rocks, my father's pond, and contests of various sorts. Once, my father suggested his own contest, requiring a tall bamboo pole, running across the front lawn, and essentially pole-vaulting some 6 feet into the air. Maybe the magic of spring protected us from becoming seriously injured that day. My older daughter, Winter, eternally a child of nature, rows on the little boat, maybe fishing, maybe sketching a water iris, maybe examining dragonfly nymphs just under the surface of the water or scooping up tiny fish with her net. Whatever she does is sure to draw in her grandfather.

While I observe these tender interactions and attempt to wax poetic about the season in my own way through photography, writing, or crafts, what I really end up doing most of the time is planning and organizing. I'm planning when to harden off and transplant my seedlings, where I will build a new garden bed, what system I will use to make compost, and how I can grow a larger quantity of healthier and better-tasting vegetables. Spring to-do lists are long and those first few weeks require discipline to stay focused on one task at a time. Though factors such as air, light, and moisture all contribute to successful gardens, gardeners always strive to improve soil quality, and that is the first outdoor chore I tackle.

improving the soil

When I first started gardening, I stripped down my understanding of the perfect soil to two adjectives: light and fluffy. These words have become an annual springtime soil mantra for me. However, it's important to understand the concept behind light and fluffy. Where we live usually determines the texture of our soil and this doesn't change. Clay is clay; sand is sand. But we can change the structure of the soil to create the best growing environment for our plants. Adding compost can both lighten up clay soil as well as improve sandy soil. It is also a great source of micronutrients that can benefit the soil in any garden. Each spring, I add an organic crumbly compost to fluff up my heavy, inorganic clay soil. The resulting lighter, more granular soil has many benefits. Shortly after sowing seeds, the surface stays loose and does not crust over. Under the surface of the soil, fine breathing spaces make it easy for tender plant roots to stretch out. It is easier to cultivate. Soil with good structure will take in water readily while also having improved drainage, giving plants the best environment to grow in.

My father has been building the soil in his garden for decades and it is now very fertile and never requires extra synthetic fertilizer. For gardeners still

The little rowboat, always on call for a quick trip around the pond or a lazy afternoon fishing under the sun.

It's close to feeding time for the white geese that wander freely during the day and rest under a big weeping willow at night.

working on their soil, a good soil test will reveal the soil's pH level and what the specific soil may be lacking. Organic amendments such as blood meal, bone meal, humus, fish meal, gypsum, limestone, rock potash, seaweed meal, or pelletized chicken manure can supply any missing nutrients.

Avoiding soil compaction is another important step toward better soil. We all know the rhyme "April showers bring May flowers"; sometimes these showers also bring a too-wet garden. Never work in the garden when it is too wet as you can compact your soil by stepping on it. If you have clay soil like I do, being too eager and clomping around in the garden means you will be making bricks rather than being productive. To mitigate this problem, consider building beds that you will not need to step into, such as a traditional Chinese intensive-style garden or raised beds. Or keep planting areas narrow enough so that you can reach the center from the paths. If you must step in the planting area, consider laying a wooden board on the soil and stepping on that to avoid compacting sections of soil under your footsteps.

building a chinese intensive bed

My father's current vegetable garden encompasses about 13,000 square feet. He has spent more than twenty years landscaping this property and tending his large garden. In fact, my father has essentially created a vision of idyllic China on his current 8-acre property, 6 acres of which are a pond dotted with ducks. Similar to the peonies, large-blooming chrysanthemums, bamboo, and white geese that make up the picture-perfect elements of his home, the vegetable garden follows a Chinese style of building garden beds that farmers and home gardeners have successfully implemented for centuries.

The area where my father made his garden had relatively few rocks or other surprises in the ground. As a result, he used a traditional Chinese method to double-dig his garden. For a less laborious method of preparing a garden plot, try layering organic compost or other materials that slowly break down over time to improve the soil. Or build raised beds if your soil is very poor.

Here's how to create a Chinese intensive garden following my father's technique. With string mark off rectangular beds of desired length, with a width of about 4 feet. Leave paths about 18 inches wide between beds. Working from the paths to avoid stepping in the planting area, double-dig the soil. Begin in the first bed by digging out the top layer of soil to the depth of a shovel and move the soil into a pile near the farthest bed. Back at the first bed, loosen the second, deeper layer of soil. Move to the second bed and remove the top layer of soil. Dump this into the first bed, breaking up any clods of clay. The soil in this first garden bed will now be loosened to the depth of about two shovels, creating a planting area with loosened soil that most vegetables will be happy to grow in. This is also the time to amend the soil, if desired. Continue to dig into the deeper layer of soil in the second bed and then fill with the top layer of soil from the third bed, mixing in compost and any other organic materials to improve the soil. Continue working on all the beds in this way. To fill the last bed, use the pile of soil set aside from the first bed. Gently rake the top of each bed flat.

In my father's intensive-style garden beds, soil gets better and more fertile every year.

Whichever method you use to prepare the soil, when creating permanent beds, gardeners are able to focus on building the soil in the individual beds and resources are never wasted. For example, any soil amendments are only added to the growing areas, not lost on paths for walking on. Water is diverted to the vegetables only. Compare this to a typical in-ground or American farm-style garden which is tilled from edge to edge each year, which is broadcast fertilized, which is watered in its entirety, and which is stepped in, compacting the soil, creating a need to till later. This method not only harms the soil structure that gardeners aim to improve, but is also a waste of resources. In my father's Chinese intensive-style garden beds, energy is devoted to cultivating, digging, and watering permanent planting areas. The soil that vegetables grow in is never stepped in and gets better each year. Paths in between the garden beds provide solid ground to stand on and work from. The stable paths also offer the grandchildren fun landing pads to leap from row to row.

The loose and fertile soil created over time allows plants to build a healthier root system, which helps produce a better crop of vegetables. Deeper roots also means plants can withstand droughts. On the flip side, slightly raised beds with

gardening up

Looking back, I can clearly see my parents' chase of the American dream through the gardens they worked. The garden my sister and I picked vegetables from as toddlers encompassed the side yard of our first childhood home. Vegetables grew neatly in horizontal beds across a fairly steep, sunny slope, and a wide path bisecting the garden allowed my father to safely tend vegetables on either side. In the backyard of our next home we had a much larger in-ground garden. The two of us played an endless variety of games on and around the old mimosa tree while my father grew Asian vegetables such as garlic chives and long beans as well as tomatoes, cucumbers, and other common American vegetables. My parents moved again after I left for college. After decades of building the soil at his current property, my father's ample intensive-style garden is highly fertile and the soil is the picture of light and fluffy. Among the white geese gliding on the water, the willow trees edging the pond, and the large Asian vegetable garden tucked into the beautiful oasis, my father has created a landscape straight out of the most scenic spots in China.

healthy, well-draining soil also allow plants to thrive during periods of heavy rain. In the spring, intensive Chinese garden beds warm up more quickly. And through the season, crops are abundant because plants can be planted closer together. For the next season's crops, separate garden beds allow for planning an easy crop rotation system, which will help grow stronger plants with fewer pests and diseases.

raised garden beds

Though my father works a large, airy, sunny piece of land ideal for vegetable gardening, gardeners always find a way to make do with their environments whether they are working in modest suburban backyards, narrow strips of soil in an alleyway, or on an apartment balcony. Many years ago, when I created my first garden, I spent weeks obsessively planning and imagined a soft whoosh of spade into grassy earth upon the inaugural groundbreaking. Imagine my

While my father's grandchildren are not opposed to helping with tasks, they'd usually rather play. The garden entices young ones with all its ridges to climb, trellises to hide behind, and paths between rows to chase each other down on.

surprise to find every inch of ground in my backyard occupied by compacted clay, maple tree roots, and rocks. Like most gardeners, determination prevented me from giving up. Much sleep was lost as I delved into research and consulted with every gardener friend I could reach. I meant to make it work, despite any problems with the site and soil, and so finally, I built raised beds a few inches off the ground instead. Raised garden beds, made with any material that holds soil in—such as wooden boards, stone, or straw bales—and then filled with a good quality soil, provide a great start to a successful vegetable garden.

container gardening

Gardening can be addicting. For people like me who yearn for more and more garden space every year, growing vegetables in containers may be a solution. Though basically anything that can hold soil can grow a plant (we've seen daisies grown in old boots, black-eyed Susans in wheelbarrows, colorful peppers in window boxes), the most important criteria is that the container is large and well-draining. For more shallow-rooted vegetables such as leafy greens, I look for a container that has a large surface area so I can grow more. The container only needs to be deep enough to allow a healthy root system to develop, usually just about 8 inches or so. In contrast, root vegetables, plants that produce edible bulbs like onions, or plants with a deeper root system such as eggplants, need deeper containers. Barrels or half-barrels are great containers for big plants. Fast-growing Chinese vegetables such as radishes and lettuces, as well as larger vegetables such as peppers and soybeans are all well suited for growing in containers. Pea shoots are both fast growing and are harvested early so they can do well even crammed into a small container. The most important considerations are soil fertility and moisture. Be sure to mix some compost into your potting soil each season and fertilize regularly if desired. And because containers tend to heat up and dry out easily during hot summer days, it is necessary to stay on top of moisture needs, watering sometimes more than once a day.

making your own compost

Each spring I prepare my garden beds by weeding and topping off with homemade compost. Compost, the rich, earthy stuff commonly referred to by gardeners as "black gold," is valuable because it improves the structure and quality of soil by adding organic matter and nutrients. You can purchase bagged compost, but making your own is simple, free, and requires only patience while

fall vegetables in spring

To fill your spring garden, consider planting some of the vegetables from the fall chapter. Many cool-weather, leafy green vegetables will grow well in spring as well. The key to success is to be sure you have enough cool days for a few harvests before the weather gets hot or the days lengthen and the vegetables bolt and turn tough and bitter. Be sure to check the days-to-maturity information on your seed packets. Some other strategies include starting seeds indoors, planting in a partially shady area in the garden, and planting successively. Every vegetable will have its own special needs and tricks, so experiment and keep good notes.

the horticultural magic takes place. Compost is made from a combination of dry, high-carbon, brown materials (such as straw and dried leaves) and moist, high-nitrogen green materials (such as kitchen scraps, lawn clippings, and weeds). The proportion should be about 1 part green to 25 parts brown. Too many greens and the pile will begin to smell and attract animals; too many browns and the pile won't decompose as quickly. In my compost pile, this means that every time I add a small bucket of kitchen scraps, I add a couple pitchfork loads of straw or leaves.

With the action of decomposition, an active compost pile is slightly moist and warm, and sometimes even visibly steamy on cold days. Decomposers such as earthworms and centipedes in the pile signal good soil ecology as they digest organic material and release nutrients back into the mix. Over time, the big pile of leaves, kitchen scraps, and grass clippings gets smaller in volume as the ingredients break down. When finished, a concentrated, brown, earthy-smelling soil remains. The only evidence that your compost came from waste you might otherwise have thrown in the trash is a random banana sticker here and there.

Regularly mixing the ingredients by turning the pile with a pitchfork can speed up the process of making compost. However, the more passive method of adding to the pile and then forgetting about it will produce rich compost as well, just at a slower pace.

The best method for making compost is the one that most suits your particular gardening situation. Large covered tumblers make easy work of turning the compost. These containers generally have small holes for moisture and air to work through the compost and are a good choice for keeping pets or other animals from accessing tasty kitchen scraps. Alternatively, a three-bin system allows one bin to hold ready-to-use compost, another bin for materials to finish in, and a third bin for adding new compost materials. A number of other systems exist, including the roughest system that my brother-in-law, Todd, employs. Down near the bottom of his property, bordering the woods, is "the hole," a giant pile where he dumps his fallen tree branches, trimmings, weeds, and other organic materials. No other upkeep of the hole is required as nature knows what to do, albeit slowly. Under the haphazard pile, a fertile black soil sits ready for use whenever he needs it.

seed sowing

Spring is a busy time for gardeners but good organization is my saving grace. In my journal, I have first and last frost dates listed, plant-growing information saved, notes about past failures and successes recorded, and a garden plan for the season drawn. Cold-hardy seeds such as lettuces and radishes are in hand and ready to be sown. It's hard to believe that with a little forethought and care, each tiny seed is capable of producing large plants that can provide food for my family.

In late winter into early spring, I inventory seeds for all the different vegetables that will go into the garden. I classify them into seeds that I will start indoors and seeds that will go directly into the garden. Because I don't have an extended growing season, I start any vegetable that requires a longer growing season before fruiting, such as tropical plants, pumpkin, or most gourds, in pots indoors under grow lights while the ground outside is still too cold and wet to work. When the soil has warmed, I harden off my seedlings over the period of a week or so and then transplant them into the garden. Giving these plants a big head start helps assure that I'll get a good harvest before frost hits in the late fall.

Lettuces, most beans, and other vegetables with a shorter time to maturity can be started directly in the garden. I start some of the cold-hardy vegetables such as radishes or tatsoi in the very early spring. I am always disappointed if an unexpected snow falls a few days after I sow a few rows of greens. But reliably, shortly after the snow melts, tiny sprouts begin to appear, heralding spring at the same time that trees begin to leaf out and tulips send up flushes of strappy leaves.

After months of hibernating indoors, ideal spring workdays mean charging through the chores. The physical work is rewarding, and in a few short weeks, all kinds of wonderful things are happening above and below the ground. Spring peas and beans climbing their trellises are flowering and beginning to grow in their pods. Mizuna's lush bright green leaves highlight spring salad mixes. Watercress in the stream is at its best, and every year I anticipate my father's beef and watercress dumplings, my favorite of his many varieties of dumplings.

Spring means freshly harvested vegetables again, particularly fresh green vegetables. On many weekends, I look forward to my mom's healthy and delicious leafy greens at dinner. The only difference from week to week is the variety of the vegetable on the plate, sometimes a mild leafy green, sometimes a sharp and spicy mustard, and oftentimes my mom's favorite—tender snow pea shoots.

With some planning in the early weeks and a little work during the growing season's mildest days, spring is an energizing, rewarding, and affirming time for the gardener both outdoors and in the kitchen.

Phyllostachys edulis

bamboo shoots

MANDARIN *zhú sǔn*
CANTONESE *zuk seon*

竹
笋

My father's large stand of bamboo greets visitors with a sense of serenity as it gently sways in a wind. Every time I visit, I remember a "Lao Tzu says" piece of advice I learned as a teenager: be resilient like bamboo, which never snaps or breaks but bends and yields during times of stress, always standing back up. As a garden plant, bamboo has a bad rap but it's not quite the nemesis that people make it out to be. It's a beautiful and sustainable material for making screens, furniture, flooring, paper, yarn, and more. With his own bamboo, my father has handcrafted brooms, serving spoons, garden trellises, tomato cages, and the cheapest high-quality mulch around.

There are two types of bamboo—clumping and running. It's easy to keep clumping bamboo reasonably contained, but the running type is what may give

Bamboo is infinitely useful in the garden. Here, my father has created three different configurations of supports with tall bamboo canes.

A simple but sturdy trellis constructed for medicinal herbs to climb up.

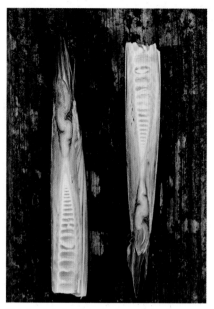

Cut shoots in half lengthwise and simply scoop out the heart with your thumbs.

pause for concern. The running type spreads by underground rhizomes. As with many plants that send runners, new bamboo rhizomes are vigorous and can run long and varying distances. My father lives on several acres and can afford to allow a large stand of bamboo to reside in a 2000-square-foot spot. For the rest of us, particularly those who have smaller yards and want to be good neighbors, it's important to be mindful of the type of bamboo we grow, where we grow it, and how to prepare for growing it.

IN THE GARDEN For many backyard gardeners, it would be wise to plant the clumping type of bamboo, or to plant bamboo in an ornamental container to prevent spreading. Another idea is to plant bamboo on high berms or mounds since new shoots will ideally run off to the side and can be spotted and pruned more easily. These methods are best for growing and containing bamboo for ornamental purposes.

To plant a larger quantity for fresh eating, it's important to take the time and care to install a metal, plastic, or concrete barrier so that running bamboo can grow in a contained space. The barrier should be at least 60 mils thick, buried into the ground to a depth of about 30 inches, and peeking out about 2 inches above the ground. Even in this case, I would urge bamboo lovers to think carefully before planting because bamboo is

Bamboo shoots are tender and abundant in the spring. A little kick breaks them off at the soil line and makes for quick and easy harvesting.

extremely difficult to remove once established.

Start a new stand of bamboo with plants or divisions. There are hundreds of varieties of bamboo, and many are edible, but the best tasting are *Phyllostachys edulis*, which can be purchased at a bamboo nursery or online. Space 3–5 feet apart so the plant will be able to send out new runners and spread. New bamboo plantings need to be watered regularly and kept from drying out. Once established, bamboo is not too fussy, and only asks for full sun. Most running types of bamboo can withstand freezes and snowy seasons, but some of the clumping types may not be hardy in colder zones. *Phyllostachys dulcis* is a great-tasting bamboo hardy in zones 6–10, and *P. praecox* (zones 7–9) and *Chimonobambusa macrophylla* (zones 7–10) have also earned high marks for taste.

Bamboo shoots are typically harvested in the spring when new shoots abound. To harvest, cut shoots when they are no more than about 8 inches tall. The portion of the shoots just under the soil line has superior flavor and nutrition, but requires more effort to harvest. To make easy work of the harvesting, do like my mom does— put on a pair of sneakers and kick the shoots one by one. They'll break off at ground level.

The harvesting period for fresh bamboo shoots is only about 2 weeks. During this time, bamboo grows fast, sometimes up to 3 feet each day. The pointy shoots grow so quickly that a funny Chinese saying always pops into my head—if out in nature and looking for a private place to relieve oneself, never go in a stand of bamboo!

IN THE KITCHEN Once harvested, it is best to eat bamboo shoots within 2 or 3 days. To prepare the long, thin shoots of running bamboo, slice in half lengthwise. Find the tip of the tender, edible heart in the center of each half, and using your thumbs, scoop the heart out of the bamboo shoot. Bamboo shoots are a mainstay in Chinese cuisine and can be sliced in stir-fry dishes and julienned in soups. My children love bamboo shoots, but only if they're my mom's freshly harvested spring shoots braised in a slightly sweet soy sauce. They don't even recognize the canned type used by restaurants as the same vegetable.

Be aware that most varieties of bamboo, including delicious edible ones, contain toxins when raw that produce cyanide in the body once ingested. To be safe, boil all freshly harvested shoots in an uncovered pan of water for about 30 minutes before using and then discard the water. This simple step quickly dissipates the toxin. What remains is a still-crisp, mild-tasting, and tender vegetable that is perfectly safe to eat and rich in nutrients. In fact, the bamboo shoot is nicknamed "king of the forest vegetables," and packs more protein than most other Asian vegetables.

BAMBOO SHOOTS AND PORK BELLY BRAISED IN SWEET SOY SAUCE

This is one of my all-time favorite comfort foods that my mom makes. It's a great recipe to double and cook on a weekend. In order to remove toxins, freshly harvested bamboo shoots must be boiled in a large pot of water for 30 minutes and then drained and rinsed in cold water before using. To use dehydrated bamboo shoots, soak in warm water for about an hour to soften. Choose pork belly with some lean streaks.

SERVES 4

1 pound pork belly, cut into 1-inch cubes

3 cups fresh bamboo shoots, peeled and precooked to remove toxins

3 tablespoons Shaoxing rice wine or sherry

5 tablespoons rock sugar (or about a 3-inch hunk)

3 tablespoons dark soy sauce

2 tablespoons light soy sauce

1 teaspoon dark (toasted) sesame oil

3 slices ginger, about ¼ inch thick

1. Place the pork belly in a small stockpot, add enough water to cover, and boil for 30 minutes. Drain and rinse the pork belly.

2. Return the pork belly to the pot along with the bamboo shoots, and add water to just cover. Then add the rice wine, sugar, dark soy sauce, light soy sauce, sesame oil, and ginger. Bring to a boil and then transfer to a Dutch oven or clay pot if desired. Cover and continue to simmer over low heat until meat is tender but not falling apart, about 1 hour.

3. If a thicker consistency is desired, increase heat and boil uncovered until the sauce reduces and thickens. Serve with steamed white rice.

Chrysanthemum coronarium

garland chrysanthemum

皇帝菜

MANDARIN *huángdì cài*
CANTONESE *wong dai choy*

There are many varieties of ornamental mums, from the hardy mum with numerous small flowers that grace North American front porches every fall, to the football type with their full and showy pompoms some 10 inches across that have been featured in Chinese art for centuries. However, one type—the edible garland chrysanthemum, *Chrysanthemum coronarium*—offers an early harvest period of aromatic greens followed by a pretty burst of small yellow or white daisy-like blooms.

Chrysanthemums are notoriously long lasting and easy to grow and it's fitting that they are the Chinese symbol of ease of life and joviality. While other common mums bloom in the fall, garland chrysanthemum produces flowers in late spring. This blooming-when-they're-not-expected-to-be-blooming phenomenon explains why they are also a symbol of auspiciousness in Chinese culture.

Harvest garland chrysanthemum in the spring when greens are tender and mild. Blooms appear in late spring.

asian greens

In the Chinese vegetable garden, all cool weather–loving leafy greens can be grown in the spring. However, Asian greens can be particular and sometimes it seems that just about any change in growing conditions can cause them to send up their tall flower stalks and go to seed, usually turning the greens bitter and unusable. Many greens tend to thrive for a longer harvest period when grown in the fall.

For eating as greens, look for plants or seeds specifically marked garland chrysanthemum, chrysanthemum greens, or crown daisy. The common flowering ornamental mum is not edible. Garland chrysanthemum is rich in vitamins A and B and contains many antioxidants. It can be used to help soothe sore throats and is often wilted in soups. In traditional Chinese medicine, garland chrysanthemum is known as an immune system booster and practitioners often recommend a tonic drink blended from the greens, nuts, and fruits—not much different from the Western version of a green smoothie that might be made of kale and fruits.

When we go out for dim sum, we always ask for a pot of tea steeped from the smaller, yellow or white *Chrysanthemum morifolium* blooms. The distinctly fragrant tea, served with a small dish of rock sugar, is sweet with an herbal fragrance. The tea and the greens, though from different species of chrysanthemums, share a similar pleasant herbal flavor.

IN THE GARDEN Chrysanthemum greens are easy to grow. They like a sunny spot, but will tolerate partial shade. In the early spring, sow seeds directly in the garden about 2 inches apart, ¼ inch deep, and in rows about 18 inches apart. Beginning when the plants are about 5 inches tall, roughly 4 weeks after planting, harvest simply by cutting the entire plant.

To have a continuous harvest, it may be a good idea to plant successively. Once the summer heat sets in, taste the leaves before using because they can become bitter. At that point, you can decide to pull the plants out to make room for another crop of greens for the fall, or leave the plants in the garden. Remaining plants that have flowered will set seed and then

Fragrant garland chrysanthemum greens are excellent in a salad mix or in light soups.

dry up. Late summer is a good time for planting more chrysanthemum greens for a fall crop, when they will grow trouble-free until frost and will taste excellent.

IN THE KITCHEN Like most Asian greens, garland chrysanthemum is usually cooked, but you can also eat the leaves raw in salads mixed with other greens. If you'll be cooking the greens, be sure to harvest much more than you think you can eat. This tendency to wilt down when cooked earned garland chrysanthemum its sarcastic Chinese nickname of "king lettuce": a big basket of fresh greens may look like something grand, but once cooked down (or stripped of jewels and robes), it ends up being a far smaller portion to eat.

Blanch, stir-fry, or steam garland chrysanthemum greens, but whichever method you choose, avoid overcooking the leaves or they may become bitter. Because of the rather distinct flavor of the leaves, garland chrysanthemum is most often enjoyed in soups or hot pots in which the leaves are added at the end of the cooking time. A classic and simple use is to create a light chicken or vegetable broth, flavor it with a few slices of ginger, and add coarsely chopped greens just before serving. Young tender stems can also be eaten, but they may require a slightly longer cooking time. If using stems and greens in the same dish, start cooking the stems first, and when near tender, add the leaves. The whole process doesn't take long.

Allium tuberosum

garlic chives

韭菜

MANDARIN *jiǔcài*
CANTONESE *gao choy*

Early in spring, the garden is dormant save for the lush green clumps of Chinese garlic chives. This is when the skinny, flat leaves of the perennial plant begin to once again stretch out after a period of winter slumber. Unlike the common chive, *Allium schoenoprasum,* which is used more sparingly as an herb, garlic chives are eaten like a vegetable in Chinese cuisine.

    This healthy vegetable contributes fiber, protein, vitamins A and C, folates, and beta-carotene to the diet. Garlic chives are a medicinal plant in traditional Chinese medicine and are considered warming to the body. Believed to have antibacterial and antifungal properties, garlic chives have also been crushed and applied to the skin to help heal wounds for centuries.

Flowering chives are harvested for their sturdy stems topped with unopened buds.

Garlic chive flowers are a pretty sight in the garden, but chives will taste grassy and are unusable at this stage. Fall will bring a few more tender harvests.

Flowering chives are also extremely popular in Chinese cuisine. They are simply the thin flowering garlic chive stems topped with tightly folded buds, which are eaten along with the stem. While garlic chives are a softer vegetable, the flowering chive stems have a sturdier structure, and are cut into shorter lengths. They hold up well in a stir-fry. If, like me, your preference is for the flowering stems, plant a flowering variety of garlic chives like 'Tai Jiu' that will tend to bloom earlier, yield more abundantly, and produce tender stems.

IN THE GARDEN Garlic chives are excellent to eat during two seasons: early spring and mid-to-late fall. Gardeners typically harvest garlic chives only through spring and then let the plants spread through summer, when leaves tend to get tough and taste grassy. Although they're not used during the height of the summer, garlic chives are perennials that do keep their fresh good looks throughout the growing season. They would be a good choice to plant in a container, where they might resemble liriope grass, with a bonus of pretty, white flowers around late summer.

In early fall, when the weather begins to cool, the entire plant should be cut at ground level. The next flush of growth will yield tender chives, which you can harvest by cutting to the soil line once again. There should be enough time to get two or three cuttings to the table before frost hits and chives disappear again until early spring.

The easiest way to start your own crop of garlic chives is by asking a friend for a division. Similar to liriope grass, a clump can be cut in half and planted in the garden where it will slowly spread. Germinating seeds is a slower process. The best way to go about it is by starting a crop of chives by seed that will grow this gardening season and be ready for harvest the next. To begin, use fresh seed and start plants indoors in late spring or summer. A heat mat will help seeds germinate quickly. In late summer or early fall, when plants are 4–6 inches tall, transplant into the garden. Choose a spot where the perennial plant can grow and be well situated for years. A sunny area in the garden is best, though chives can tolerate some light shade. Plant each seedling about 2 inches deep so that the base of the plant is below the soil line. Chives do well when grown in clumps, so plant six to ten seedlings per clump and situate the clumps 8–10 inches apart.

Keep plants well watered until established. Growth may be slow at first, but after a period of dormancy in the winter, plants will take off. When chives are about 6 inches tall, harvest by either cutting a handful of leaves at a time, or by cutting the whole clump. When cutting, try to aim right at the soil line because the lighter-colored base of the plant is the most tender part.

You can produce tender yellow chives by depriving them of light while growing.

To produce yellow chives, simply cut the entire clump of green chives, and then allow the next flush of leaves to grow deprived of light. You can do this by growing them under dark row covers, covering with pots, or simply earthing up the soil so that light does not reach the leaves. Because the plant grows vigorously in a cut-and-come-again fashion through a long season, it's common for gardeners to alternate a green crop of chives with a blanched yellow crop for variety. Yellow chives should be eaten within a day or two of harvesting or they will begin to wilt.

IN THE KITCHEN In our family, the garlicky-oniony flavor of chopped Chinese chives (*gao choy* in Cantonese) harkens spring in my father's expertly folded pork and chive steamed buns. Chives are also used to flavor stir-fries, noodle dishes, or soups. They are often added toward the end of the cooking time as they can get tough if overcooked.

Blanched yellow chives (*gao choy wong* in Cantonese) are milder in flavor and are a delicacy enjoyed for their tender leaves. We have a local restaurant that serves yellow chives as a condiment alongside plum sauce with their Peking duck. I also love when my mom makes a clear chicken broth flavored with a dash of fish sauce, sesame oil, and yellow chives. Nestled in this soup are her

Hong Kong–style wontons filled with minced pork and big bites of shrimp.

My personal favorite is the garlic-flavored flowering chive (*gao choy fa* in Cantonese). A more substantial vegetable, it is delicious stir-fried along with other vegetables, meat, or seafood. Whichever type of chive you try, rinse well before using as the base of the plants can be gritty.

STIR-FRIED FLOWERING CHIVE WITH ROASTED DUCK

It's hard to reproduce a glistening, restaurant-roasted, crisp-skinned duck at home, so this simple recipe uses the breast of a restaurant-bought whole roasted duck. The subtle garlicky flavor of the flowering chives and the salty succulent duck are a match like no other. Fresh flowering chives are tender and only require a few minutes of cooking time. To prepare the chives, remove any part of the bottom of the stem that is flexible. Freshly harvested flowering chive stems should be crisp and snap when broken. As much as we all love this recipe, we equally enjoy eating the leftover duck the next day, sometimes cut up and atop soup with white noodles; duck bone broth is also excellent.

SERVES 4

1 roasted duck breast, skin on, from a 5-pound whole roasted duck

1 tablespoon corn or peanut oil

2 tablespoons hoisin sauce

½ pound flowering chive stems, cut into 1-inch segments

½-inch section ginger, cut into a few slices

1. Cut duck breast into 2-inch sections, then julienne.

2. Place a wok over medium-high heat. When hot, add the oil, hoisin sauce, and duck. Stir-fry for about a minute. Add the chives and ginger and cook until chive stems are tender, 2–5 minutes.

Pisum sativum var. *saccharatum* (snow pea)
Pisum sativum var. *macrocarpon* (sugar snap pea)

snow peas and sugar snap peas

MANDARIN *hélán dòu, tiándòu*
CANTONESE *ho laan dao, teem dao*

荷
蘭
豆

甜
豆

My mom likes beans of all kinds, but she is particularly fond of snow peas and sugar snap peas, two vegetables with edible pods. Snow peas are flat pods that contain small, barely developed pea seeds; sugar snaps are crisp bulging pods filled with a row of peas. Both are slightly sweeter than fresh garden peas and don't require the extra work of shelling.

Snow peas and sugar snaps are popular additions to mixed vegetable combinations in Chinese restaurant stir-fry dishes. These healthy vegetables are rich in fiber, protein, vitamins C and K, folates, iron, and antioxidants. They are believed to have anti-inflammatory properties and are recommended by nutritionists to people with asthma, autoimmune diseases, and arthritis for relief of symptoms.

IN THE GARDEN Snow peas and sugar snaps are relatively easy to grow and have similar growing requirements. Sow seeds directly in the garden in the early spring. Peas are tolerant of cold, wet ground and will germinate when outside temperatures are as low as 40 degrees Fahrenheit. Plant seeds about 1/2 inch deep and thin to stand about 5 inches apart. Pea plants love to stretch and will need some sort of support to stay upright. To grow strong healthy plants, try planting seeds in a trench and as the plants grow, build the soil up so that the soil line eventually covers the first few inches of the plant.

Snow peas can be picked when the flat pods are still immature. Like other peas, snow pea plants grow vigorously. 'Oregon Sugar Pod II' is a popular variety that will be ready in about 68 days. During the height of the harvest season in late spring, peas will need to be picked regularly. Too many pods left to dry on the plant will signal the plant to stop producing.

Pick sugar snaps when the peas

Sugar snaps are enjoyed for their sweet peas inside and their crisp outer pod. Many people prefer to remove the strings, but you can leave them on if picked at their prime while still tender.

fill out in their pods. You can harvest them before this stage if desired, but those who like the plump peas inside the pods will want to wait until they're mature.

Both types of peas will struggle when temperatures rise above 70 degrees Fahrenheit. Planting an early variety is an option for gardeners with short spring seasons. 'Norli' is a snow pea that produces petite and delicious pods ready for eating in about 50 days. 'Sugar Ann' is a popular early sugar snap variety that is usually ready about a week and a half before other sugar snaps.

IN THE KITCHEN Both snow peas and sugar snaps have strings running down either side that may be left on or removed. This is a matter of preference. However, especially as they

Snow peas are flat edible pods with just barely formed peas inside. They are nutritious and versatile in the kitchen.

The edible pods of sugar snaps have a crisp texture and are excellent stir-fried.

mature, strings can become tough and hard to chew, so most people prepare the vegetable by cutting the tip and then zipping the string off before cooking.

Stir-fried, steamed, or blanched until crisp-tender and tossed in a cold salad—both types of peas add vibrant color and texture to any recipe. To keep up with a large harvest, pick the mild, sweet pods often, blanch the pods to retain the bright green color, drain well, and then freeze for later use.

MIXED VEGETABLE CHOW FUN

In a good Chinese restaurant these soft noodles will be speckled with a few spots of brown, and the entire dish will be infused with a slight smokiness accomplished by a professional kitchen's super hot flames. In the home kitchen, we can re-create this by resisting the urge to stir immediately and frequently and by letting the noodles cook undisturbed for a bit. The wide rice noodles used in this dish are generally sold pre-cooked in Asian supermarkets, either fresh in the bakery section or bagged in the refrigerator case. Ask for *haw fun*. Much of any season's garden harvest can go into the combination of vegetables used in this recipe. The trick is to separate the harder vegetables (such as sugar snaps, carrots, baby corn, green beans, and the sturdy stems of Chinese greens) from the softer vegetables (such as bean sprouts, mushrooms, and tops of leafy greens) because the harder vegetables require a longer cooking time. Vegetarians can look for a vegetarian oyster sauce, usually made from mushrooms. If you choose to add chicken or sliced beef, stir-fry the meat first, set aside in a bowl, then add to the wok of cooked vegetables at the end to reheat just before topping the plate of cooked noodles.

SERVES 4-6

2 tablespoons light soy sauce

2 teaspoons cornstarch

2 teaspoons Shaoxing rice wine

2 tablespoons oyster sauce

½ cup water

3–5 tablespoons corn or peanut oil

1 pound fresh wide rice noodles, cut into ¾-inch strips and then separated

4 slices ginger, ¼ inch thick

3 green onions, cut into 2-inch lengths

4 cups vegetables, rinsed (any combination of sugar snaps, snow peas, long beans cut into 2-inch sections, bean sprouts, julienned carrots, mushrooms, baby corn, or Chinese greens such as bok choy or gailan cut into 2-inch sections)

1 teaspoon minced garlic

1. Combine the soy sauce, cornstarch, rice wine, oyster sauce, and water in a glass or small bowl. Set aside.

2. Heat a wok over high heat until hot and then add 2 or 3 tablespoons of oil. When hot, add the separated noodles and quickly spread them along the walls of the wok. Cook for 30 seconds without stirring. Then, gently turn and stir noodles until they're softened, about 5 minutes. Transfer to a serving dish.

3. Reduce heat to medium heat and add another 1 or 2 tablespoons of oil to the wok. When hot, add the ginger and green onions and stir until fragrant, about 1 minute. Add sugar snaps and other hard vegetables and stir-fry for about 5 minutes, stirring occasionally. Add remaining softer vegetables and garlic. Continue to cook until all vegetables are tender, about 3 more minutes.

4. Add the soy sauce mixture to the wok and cook until the sauce bubbles and thickens. Pour the mixed vegetables and sauce over the noodles to serve.

Pisum sativum var. *saccharatum*

snow pea shoots

豆苗

MANDARIN *dòumiáo*
CANTONESE *dao miu*

Many people have had snow peas in mixed vegetable combinations or in various dishes in Chinese restaurants. However, the pea shoot is the real specialty found on the menus handed exclusively to the Chinese customers at the most authentic Chinese restaurants. In Asian and international markets, the delicate, beautiful, and delicious shoots are always more expensive than the pea pods. When grown at home, gardeners can benefit by enjoying shoots earlier in the season and then pods a few weeks later.

The mild-flavored, tender snow pea shoot, *dao miu* in Cantonese, has always been my mother's favorite vegetable. I think part of the allure is the fresh green color, beautifully shaped immature pea leaves, shoot tips, tendrils, and occasional flowers.

Pea shoots, similar to microgreens, contain more nutrition than their mature counterparts. Extremely high in vitamins A and C, folates, and beta-carotene, this easy-to-use, versatile, and delicious vegetable is a nutritional powerhouse. The shoots of any type of pea can be grown for eating, but we like the characteristics of snow pea shoots best. They are also the shoots most commonly found in Asian supermarkets and restaurants.

IN THE GARDEN I have two plans for growing pea shoots. The first plan is an ambitious one that aims to produce enough for a couple cuttings of fresh pea shoots, along with some beautiful, flat, green pods to eat later as well. Snow pea plants are easy to grow and are tolerant of cold, wet ground. In early spring, sow seeds directly in the garden about ½ inch deep and about 5 inches apart. Snow peas like to climb and will need some sort of support to stay upright. Once plants are established at about 2 feet tall, you can harvest the shoots by pinching off the top 6 inches or so of the plant right above a light-colored growing tip. All parts of the plant are edible and delicious. About 3 weeks later, new shoots can be taken off the top. Plants continue to grow and flower and in a few more weeks, will produce pods that can be harvested shortly thereafter.

Alternatively, I grow pea shoots for the sole purpose of harvesting the tender greens. For this plan, sow seeds closer together in the garden. As soon as the shoots are about 1 foot tall, harvest the top 6 inches or so. Another harvest will be ready in 3–4 weeks. Keep harvesting until the greens begin to get tough with the heat of the summer. This would be a great plan for balcony or container gardeners, or even gardeners who grow vegetables indoors under grow lights. Another crop can be started in the fall. Some may argue that fall is when pea shoots are at their best, especially when these fairly hardy greens are hit with a light frost and gain a touch of sweetness.

IN THE KITCHEN Raw or cooked, snow pea shoots go well in just about any recipe that calls for a mild and delicate green like spinach. In Chinese cuisine, snow pea shoots are usually quickly stir-fried and always just lightly seasoned. They only require a few minutes of cooking time and are ready to eat as soon as the thickest part of the stems are tender. Because pea shoots are somewhat sweet and mild, they're best when not in the shadow of too many other ingredients or strong flavors.

My mom's favorite way to cook *dao miu* is super fast, nutritious, and delicious. Simply stir-fry or blanch shoots for a few minutes until slightly wilted and hot, and then drain and toss with some soy sauce and sesame oil.

Sweet and delicate pea shoots are eaten stem, leaves, flowers, tendrils, and all.

Nasturtium officinale

watercress

MANDARIN *xīyán caì*
CANTONESE *sai yeong choy*

西洋菜

Watercress is one of the earliest spring greens available on my father's bucolic property. With a gently trickling stream flowing into his pond under dappled sunlight, he has the ideal environment for a happy, permanent planting of watercress. Watercress spreads plentifully and thrives with few pests or diseases, yet we still race the geese and ducks for the best of the spring harvest.

Peppery, leafy green watercress has been cultivated since ancient times and has been historically used as a health food as well. Rich in vitamin C, antioxidants, and minerals like calcium, and also having a crisp, slightly bitter flavor, watercress has always been popular with both health fanatics and gourmets. A semi-aquatic plant, watercress stays fresh in stores for only a short period of time, so a gardener's own fresh harvest is always a special springtime treat.

IN THE GARDEN Watercress is a perennial plant and hardy in most zones. To establish watercress, choose a site in sun to partial shade and in an area with fresh, gently flowing water. Look for plants at farmer's markets, nurseries, or online sources. Plant watercress along the banks of your stream about 6 inches apart so that the leaves sit just at or above the surface of the water. It may be necessary to place some pebbles or small rocks around the plants to hold them in place underwater. Little more is needed to establish a crop of watercress. To harvest, simply cut what you need. Watercress will re-grow and can typically be cut at least a couple of times each spring. Spring harvests tend to produce the mildest, yet still flavorful, greens.

Don't have a flowing stream with ideal growing conditions? Some gardeners have been able to successfully grow watercress in containers. If you want to give this a try, use a rich soil and keep the soil consistently damp at all times. However, while watercress likes moisture, it will not do well in standing water. Planting in a container, as opposed to planting directly in the garden, can help you control

Watercress is at its best when planted in a gently flowing stream under dappled sunlight.

root your own watercress

An easy source for finding watercress may be the Asian supermarket where you can root your own plants to grow. Buy a bunch of the freshest-looking watercress and place it in a cup of water to root. In a few weeks, roots will be several inches long and ready for planting.

Spring watercress is tender and slightly peppery, an excellent addition to salad greens.

mizuna

Looking to add some more interest to your salad? Mizuna (*Brassica rapa* Japonica Group) is a beautiful, feathery Japanese leafy green with foliage so bright and showy that some gardeners plant it in flowerbeds. It is also a good source of beta-carotene, calcium, and vitamin C. Being both cold and wet tolerant, mizuna's growth is not hindered by unexpected late frosts. In the early spring, directly sow seeds in the garden. Once plants are taller than 5 inches tall or so, harvest outer leaves as needed or cut the entire plant about an inch from the soil line. Mizuna will quickly re-grow and be ready for another cutting in just a few weeks. A relative of mustard greens, mizuna has just enough bite to spice up a spring salad mix and is delicious raw or cooked or as an alternative to arugula. It can also be lightly stir-fried or placed in the bottom of a bowl before ladling hot soup over top. Though it is commonly known as a Japanese vegetable, mizuna's origins can be traced to China where it is known as *shui choy*, meaning water vegetable, which refers to its juicy stalks.

and stay vigilant about the moist growing conditions that are required. I've seen watercress grown successfully in flats, pots, small ponds, and even old wading pools and sandboxes.

IN THE KITCHEN Watercress is often eaten raw in North America and adds a nice tang to spring salad mixes. In Chinese cuisine, watercress is usually cooked before eating. The tender greens need just a few minutes of cooking in a hot pan to wilt and they taste great alone as a side dish topped with sautéed garlic. Watercress is also excellent in noodle dishes, or as an accompaniment to meat or fish dishes.

I like watercress best as a bed for steamed minced beef balls (made with a pinch of orange zest and Worcestershire sauce) and in my father's beef and watercress dumplings. Beef and watercress is a classic combination, but the greens also make an easy substitute for most Asian greens or slightly peppery or bitter lettuces such as arugula or radicchio.

SUMMER

夏
天

Summer is when family and friends of my parents are particularly excited to see my father, for he often greets them with bags of freshly harvested vegetables. Having honed his skills from a lifetime of farming for survival and then gardening for pleasure, his expertise in growing vegetables makes summer a time of abundant harvests with greens, squashes, fruits, and even fish and eggs to share with his lucky circle of friends.

Years ago, my parents invited their friend John and his family over for dinner. John was a successful businessman, and like my parents, originally from the province of Shandong. He spent his ▸

Granddaughters picking from the rows of tomatoes that grow among the Chinese vegetables in my father's garden.

Pink water lilies in my father's pond signal the beginning of summer.

entire adult life in America. As he often does, my father made dumplings for dinner. That night they were filled with summer squash, shrimp, and pork belly, and seasoned with rice wine, soy sauce, and sesame oil. My father's dumplings are always incredible—folded into fat, nearly bursting purses, with thin skins that somehow never break open, and juicy flavorful fillings that change throughout the year, depending upon what's in season. But on this night, John didn't just compliment my father like a typical polite dinner guest; John cried. Turns out, having lost his mother as a boy, and having left Shandong at a young age, John had a taste of memories from long, long ago. Something in the combination of ingredients and my father's old-fashioned dumpling-making skills transported him back to childhood in China. Food can do that in an instant.

John's experience is common among immigrants who taste a beloved but long-forgotten food from their home countries. When we work our own gardens, we are able to experiment with new vegetables, but also seek out old favorites. While I try several new varieties of heirloom tomatoes each year, I also make space to grow traditional vegetables such as long beans or luffa gourds, which I use to experiment with my mom's recipes. Sometimes I grow Chinese vegetables just to connect in some symbolic way with the ancestors I never knew.

summer pests

Along with some Chinese vegetables, bumper crops of peppers and squash, a thriving herb garden, and baskets of sun-warmed tomatoes on the kitchen table are what a good summer looks like to me. The bright ripe fruits in the garden always pique the interest of my husband who likes to brainstorm new ways to use them, usually involving the grill. For me, summer also tests my will to overcome my garden failures due to a host of problems such as drought, slugs, hornworms, squash bugs, blight, sunscald, and—I will be the first to admit—an annual case of summertime neglect.

May into June, things seem to go swimmingly. Gourd plants are sending out big leaves on thick stems. Beans are climbing supports and we may have even begun picking. Eggplants are dotted with purple flowers. But what's this? Upon closer inspection, I notice that the eggplant leaves are riddled with tiny pinholes—my first sign that the battle with the flea beetle has begun. In my garden, insect pests are typically the first sign of decline. And of course, the same insects that attack my non-Chinese vegetables also attack my Chinese vegetables.

I inevitably make my way to the gardening aisle of every store I enter, reading the backs of pesticide spray bottles. But after weighing the pros and cons of each product, I snap out of wanting to take the easy way out and quickly walk away knowing that there are better strategies to beat the damage done by pests without resorting to a chemical spray. My ancestors did without these chemicals after all, and they grew all the food they consumed. Most of these sprays kill insects indiscriminately. While a spray may effectively wipe out all the aphids in its stream, it may also kill any nearby ladybugs or other beneficial insects that would have done the favor for you in due time.

Many home gardeners practice integrated pest management, a minimal-use, environmentally sensitive method of controlling pests that pairs information about the life cycles of pests with, when necessary, other forms of pest control. Incidentally, Chinese gardeners have been practicing integrated pest management for centuries. Keen observation is part of this method. They learn quickly

Garlic chive flowers attract insects, many of which are beneficial to the garden.

which insects are damaging and understand their habits. They know about practices that either discourage their presence, or cause their demise. Beneficial lacewings, for example, are bred to lay their eggs on coils of newspaper, which may then be placed out in the fields to eventually kill aphids. Growers collect ant nests and place them strategically on fruit trees in order to control a range of insect pests. In rural areas of China, successful gardeners depend on sharing this kind of knowledge. Illustrated manuals are common and most gardeners, even in remote areas, are able to identify true garden pests, as well as garden friends. Recently, my father showed me some chewed out leaf damage near the tips of some of his single-stemmed bunching onions. He ripped the top few inches off of a large hollow onion leaf to reveal a small black beetle making a nice home inside. He explained that he's watched as this particular type of beetle chews a tiny, almost undiscoverable entryway near the top of the onion, burrows inside, and begins to feed off of the leaves. It takes about a week before the leaf damage becomes noticeable. It is only through the investment of time and patience in the garden that gardeners gain clues about pests and problems. By watching carefully, we can learn when we have a problem to contend with, and what insects living in the garden we can reasonably tolerate.

As a gardener who had been eating organically for most of my lifetime, it was important for me to learn what it meant to garden organically. In my days as a new gardener, I remember posting a photo of an imperfect vegetable on an imperfect plant in a gardening forum in order to elicit advice and being told, "I love the way an organic garden looks." It took a while to understand this was not sarcasm. A vegetable grown organically does not always look perfectly shaped and colored as it does on a supermarket shelf. An organic vegetable may have a blemish or two. Its leaves may have a few holes, and that is all okay.

When I first started gardening and an infestation presented itself, it was difficult to know which insects were harmful to my vegetables and which were supposed to be a happy sight in the garden. In a natural cycle, a large presence of damaging insects is often followed by the onslaught of beneficial insects that take care of business for us. It'd be nice if we could tell whether they were good or bad guys by the way they look. But sometimes innocuous-looking pests like slugs can do a great deal of damage, while a more formidable-looking insect, such as a wasp, may be beneficial to the garden.

Prevention is an important part of pest management. For gardeners, this means building quality soil in order to raise healthy plants that are less susceptible to attack by damaging insects. Knowing about seasonal cycles and local conditions is part of good prevention. In my region, I know that aphids do most damage in the late spring when days begin to warm up. I've also noticed that my spring lettuces tend to look freshest before this period of the aphid population boom. Knowing the seasonal patterns of insects means that my friends who struggle with flea beetle damage on their spring crop of tatsoi, for example, may have better luck growing their greens in the fall instead.

Barriers such as lightweight floating row covers also keep flea beetles and other insects out. Another great method for removing insects, if you can bear it, is to simply pick them off. Spend time with your plants and learn to identify damaging insects. Then protect your plants from further damage by squishing eggs under leaves, picking off bugs that do harm, drowning slugs, and leaving cutworms on the sidewalk for the birds to pick up.

Good hygiene plays a big role in preventing damaging insect infestations. Not only are Chinese gardens well organized, but they are typically meticulously clean as well. My father weeds often and composts spent vegetables promptly, which means fewer places for pests and slugs to infest or winter over in. Planning vegetables to grow in a rotation can also help limit damage done by pests that have overwintered in the soil. For example, if you grew brassicas in a certain bed last year, and cabbage moths became a nuisance, the pests may be overwintering in the soil. Plant your brassicas in a garden bed on another side of the garden this year.

garden diseases

Problems such as bacterial soft rot, mildews, damping off, and viruses pose another challenge for the gardener. In my backyard, sometimes I feel that when insects aren't chewing leaves or sucking fruits, damaging fungal spores are floating into my garden and I have to contend with yet another issue.

When conditions are favorable, plant diseases can spread quickly, and most of the time, when they are established, there is little recourse but to pull the plant and dispose of it properly so spores do not continue to spread. Do not throw these plants in the compost pile where disease can spread. And after working with diseased plants, wash hands and gardening tools. Unfortunately,

My daughter Lyric helping water plants during a late summer dry spell.

A raised lip at the base of a plant helps to catch and hold water, preserving resources.

when diseases attack, they are difficult to fight, so a big part of disease control is prevention. Like insect damage prevention, practices such as good hygiene, crop rotation, developing healthy soil, and growing strong plants will help prevent garden diseases.

watering the summer garden

The method used for watering is an important consideration in disease prevention. Try to keep backsplash to a minimum when watering. Mulching plants also helps to keep water where it belongs, at the roots of the plants. In China, farmers sometimes use a rowed ridge and furrow method of irrigation in which vegetables are planted in ridges and water collects in furrows. This system results in fewer moisture-related plant diseases.

Paradoxically, during the hot summer season, when we're not fighting

plan and plant for fall

When summer is in full swing and the focus is on how to stay cool on 90-degree days, don't forget to think about the fall garden. I always mark my calendar, otherwise I would surely miss my window of opportunity to plan for and begin sowing my early fall crops. To figure out when to start an excellent fall vegetable such as gailan (often called Chinese broccoli), look at the number of days to maturity on the seed packet. Add 2–3 weeks to account for germination time and then count backward from the average first frost date for your zone. Because seeds need to be consistently moist while germinating, and because your planting date may be on one of those hot end-of-summer days, it is important to remember to water your seedlings, even daily if necessary. Planting fall crops under a shade cloth, or behind taller summer vegetables, may help keep soil cool and conditions moist.

problems borne from too-humid conditions in my zone 6 garden, we're looking for ways to preserve moisture during dry spells. For squash and other vegetables that like to be watered frequently, my father builds a raised lip around the planting area, which helps capture rainfall and direct water to the roots of the plant.

In my father's intensive planting beds, which are built up off the ground, he sets his mustards and other greens in a slightly sunken surface so that any irrigation happens in the planting area. These vegetables have shallow root systems and like frequent watering for best growth. For other vegetables in his garden he uses the ridge and furrow method. As with pest control, it is important to have good knowledge about each plant. Rather than indiscriminately watering the whole garden every morning, learn the specific needs of what you're growing. Lettuces like frequent watering. Beans, gourds, eggplants, and other fruiting vegetables require heavy watering when flowering and when fruits are setting. Radishes and other root crops like regular watering only in the early stages.

On days that my father does need to supplement what rain generally provides him, he carries buckets of water from his 6-acre pond to his garden. The nutrients from the pond certainly act as a natural fertilizer and contribute to the health of his plants. Mornings or evenings are the best times to water the

My father's summer garden with lush greens and abundant fruits.

garden, and watering the root zone of a nicely mulched plant focuses resources.

The microclimate in my backyard garden tends to be damp and too humid, but I do have occasional dry spells. More likely than that, my garden suffers by my own hand from watering neglect, particularly during the height of the summer when the mosquitoes hold me hostage inside. Improving the soil is always critical for a successful garden, but it helps with moisture management as well. The soil in my area is made up of a lot of clay. If you can imagine watering a hunk of pure clay, you can envision the water rolling right off the surface. By improving the soil structure by adding more organic materials, the resulting soil is able to take in and hold more moisture. The same is true for the opposite type of soil. If you poured water into a pot of sand, the water would rush right through. By adding organic materials, sandy soils are able to hold more moisture as well.

A thick layer of mulch such as shredded leaves or straw helps keep the soil cool and retain moisture from rain or hand-watering. Applied several inches thick, mulch also helps keep weeds down. While there are many options for mulch that range from composted manure to plastic films, and all can be effective, I try to use a mulch like straw that will last the season but will decompose fairly quickly. As my garden mulch breaks down over time, it builds up the soil by adding organic material to the mix, increasing soil fertility.

asian garden tools

A fork hoe head fashioned on a heavy hewn length of wood, like the one at left, makes quick work of breaking up soil before planting.

My favorite handheld tools are variations of those that my ancestors used. Many tools used today are variations of age-old Chinese tools.

When weeds do get past me, I find the action of sitting in the sun, pulling weeds by hand, to be almost meditative. For those with a larger area or who prefer to save their backs, new versions of antique Chinese-style garden tools are available. Many of these tools are fixed on either short or long handles, and have a long, curved, scythe-like style to them. Like other garden hoes, they are used to cut the weed just under the soil line. Being somewhat of a minimalist, I have an affinity for old Asian tools, like the knife-shaped Japanese hori-hori tool. I use it as an all-in-one tool to cut, dig, mark, plant, and weed.

weeds

Mulching is also probably the best method for controlling weeds. A thick cover of mulch prevents weed seeds from ever seeing the light of day. For those weeds that do come up, I find weeding just after a rain allows me to hand pull with ease. Weeds typically fall under two categories: perennial or annual. Perennial weeds come back year after year and usually have deep taproots or runners that need to be dug completely out. Annual weeds finish their lifecycle within a year, but most are tenacious, creating thousands of tiny seeds each season. These seeds fall right back into the soil or can be blown away or carried to new locations by animals. They can then sit underground beneath inches of soil, sometimes viable for years, just waiting to be uncovered by a gardener. It is important to pull annual weeds before they have a chance to flower and set more seed. Diligent weeding every year does have a cumulative effect as the quantity of weed seeds in the ground lessens. Being persistent will result in fewer weeds as the years pass.

In a Chinese intensive-style garden bed like my father's, weeds have a slimmer chance for survival. The garden area is more focused, so weeds are easier to spot. Also, the typical practice of spacing plants a little closer together creates a canopy that prevents weed seeds from blowing in and shades out any new weeds that attempt to grow.

Each summer, I labor away weeding, laying mulch, lugging pail after pail of water from the rain barrel to the garden, inspecting, observing, and worrying about my fruits and vegetables. Summer seems to be a time when the season's challenges determine a gardener's fate. Will I give up? Or will I research a problem, talk to other gardeners, try new methods, or at least resolve to give it a go again next year? Persistence and perseverance tend to produce the best results, leading to a better garden every year with new practices discovered. Most gardeners I've met would never describe themselves as experts because there is always more to learn, and always new ideas to try. Summer is a time for both learning how to become a better gardener, and for reaping the literal fruits of all the hard work done and faith kept in the months prior.

Amaranthus tricolor

amaranth

莧菜

MANDARIN *xiàncài*
CANTONESE *yeen choy*

Plants known as amaranth are made up of a wide variety of species, each valued for different purposes and with variations in colored blooms, leaves, and forms. One of the showiest varieties of amaranth is the ornamental love-lies-bleeding. Vegetable amaranth is just as popular among different civilizations around the world, but for eating. I once had it at a restaurant in St. Lucia where the West Indians use it for callaloo, a popular local greens dish. Sometimes vegetable amaranth is called Chinese spinach; although this is not botanically correct, the leaves can be used like spinach.

In China, vegetable amaranth's pretty green, or green-and-red variegated, leaves are harvested all summer. For gardeners, after a long season of eating the mild greens, the ornate flowers are a great bonus. Amaranth was once touted as the "crop of the future" because it is inexpensive to produce, highly nutritious,

A beautiful red and green variety of vegetable amaranth, also known as Chinese spinach and often sold as 'Red Leaf'.

Amaranth is one of a few beautiful leafy green vegetables that can really take the heat of the summer.

water spinach

Water spinach (*Ipomoea aquatica*), *ong choy* in Cantonese, has long hollow stems and thin, arrow-shaped leaves. It grows in many parts of China and throughout Asia, but this semi-aquatic tropical vine particularly thrives in Southeast Asia. It is a tender, mild-tasting, popular green vegetable believed to have properties that can help cure jaundice, anemia, and liver problems, probably due to the high level of antioxidants in the plants. Water spinach is also packed with vitamins A and C, calcium, iron, and protein. My Southeast Asian friends, who call it *kangkong*, enjoy eating these fresh greens for many months. It is traditionally paired with the hot and pungent flavors of chile peppers and dried shrimp (try a small amount of fermented tofu for a vegetarian rendition). The plant spreads so abundantly in hot and wet environments that farmers in Asia have plenty to share with the ducks, chickens, and pigs. However, the United States Department of Agriculture has listed water spinach as a federal noxious weed and it is illegal to grow in some states. If you should find water spinach seed, be sure to research the rules in your region first and always plant with caution.

and can also be eaten as a whole grain or ground into a gluten-free flour. Vegetable amaranth leaves have more than twice the iron of spinach and are high in calcium. In traditional Chinese medicine the greens are said to improve blood circulation and have a cooling effect on the body.

Amaranth is my father's favorite vegetable because he likes the smooth texture of the cooked greens. It is my sister's favorite Chinese leafy green as well, but she's found the amaranth greens available at her Asian grocer to be too tough. Now she depends on her balcony garden harvest to enjoy these tender greens fresh.

IN THE GARDEN You'll find amaranth seeds in the ornamental pages of a catalog but it's important to plant an edible variety if you plan to eat the greens. Because so many different varieties are available, each with their own subtleties in taste, texture, and form, I recommend trying a few types

Mild-tasting vegetable amaranth is a quick-cooking leafy vegetable. This red-colored variety bleeds red as it cooks.

to find your favorite. We grow a family heirloom variety with small, round, green and red leaves that closely resembles 'Red Leaf' amaranth.

When the soil warms, sow seeds directly in the garden about ¼ inch deep, and space according to seed packet instructions. As plants grow, pinch the tops regularly to keep flowers from forming. You can harvest the outer leaves when plants are about 8 inches tall. Most varieties of vegetable amaranth will grow 2–3 feet tall; provide support if plants begin to get floppy. I love amaranth because when many greens have bolted in the heat of summer, amaranth is still thriving.

Near the end of the summer, leave the plant to flower for ornamental arrangements or if you have a great quantity, for harvesting the seeds for cooking. To save seeds, hang the cut

seedhead upside down in a paper bag until completely dry. Commercially grown amaranth sold as grains in markets are usually grown from *Amaranthus cruentus*, *A. hypochondriacus*, or *A. caudatus*.

IN THE KITCHEN You can substitute amaranth in any recipe that calls for cooked spinach. Most people cook amaranth before eating; try steaming it in the small amount of water remaining on the leaves after rinsing. Keep in mind that amaranth greens cook very quickly and can get mushy if cooked too long. In Chinese cuisine, amaranth is often chopped and simply allowed to wilt in a soup broth or lightly stir-fried as a vegetable side dish. Varieties with red coloring will often bleed red when cooked.

Momordica charantia

bitter melon

MANDARIN *kǔguā*
CANTONESE *fu gwaa, leong gwaa*

苦瓜 涼瓜

Fans of this aptly named gourd recognize bitter melon by its bright green, bumpy skin. The Chinese bitter melon can be distinguished from its Indian cousin by its longer shape and more smoothed out bumps; the smaller Indian bitter melon has pointed ends and almost warty bumps. Both types are enjoyed for their health benefits and distinct taste. To brace first-timers, consider other desirable bitter tastes in the culinary world such as dark chocolate, grapefruit,

Everyone should try bitter melon at least once. The beautiful bumpy fruit is touted as having numerous health benefits.

and vodka—bitter melon is the sophisticated bitter food of the fruiting vegetable family. Those who love bitter melon might speak of the bitter tang or the refreshingly cooling quality of the bitterness. The taste is hard to describe so you must try it for yourself at least once. Bitter melon is believed to lower blood glucose and lipid levels and has been found to have antiviral and antioxidant properties. In fact, especially regarding its benefit to diabetics, bitter melon has been dubbed the "magic melon."

'Hong Kong Green' is similar to the variety my family grows. These 8- to 10-inch fruits are a bright green color and have relatively smooth bumps. It is widely grown in Canton and Southeast Asia and is the bitter melon used in the Cantonese cuisine that I grew up eating. Today a white variety called 'White Pearl' is available in Asian supermarkets and seed catalogs. While my parents prefer the taste of the green Cantonese bitter melon, the pure white variety, popular in Taiwan, is quite a beauty and would be a great one to try as well.

IN THE GARDEN Growing Chinese bitter melon requires some attention at the outset because the plant has a longer germination period, sometimes up to 30 days. Soaking the seed for a couple of hours in lukewarm water or nicking the thick seed coat prior to sowing your seeds may help speed the germination process. It is possible to directly seed in the garden, but the soil must be warm (about 70 degrees Fahrenheit) or the seed may rot before a cotyledon ever sees the light of day. A soil thermometer can help determine when it is a good time to sow seeds or transplant seedlings. For gardeners without an exceptionally long growing season, it may be wise to start bitter melon from seed indoors several weeks before the last frost date.

Once established, the bitter melon vine will love a sunny spot in the garden with an 8-foot-tall structure to climb up and over. Despite being a climber, the vine will never grow out of control. Begin harvesting approximately 60 days after planting out—a slight smoothing out of the bumpy ridges indicates that the melons are ripe. Pick the fruits while they're still green and 6–12 inches long. To save seed, allow a couple of robust gourds to yellow on the vine. Then, either use your favorite seed-saving method or allow nature to take over in its unique way with bitter melon.

At a later stage of maturity, the melons will split open on their own, displaying individual seeds covered in bright red, goopy mucilage. At this point, you can collect the seeds and rinse them off, or you can leave them on the plant or even allow them to drop to the ground. Ants and other insects will carry the mucilage off and you'll be able to collect your seeds the next day. The red goop is sweet and edible. In fact, when my father was a boy, he grew bitter melon expressly

Bitter melon requires a tall structure for vines to climb. Midsummer, fruits hang down for picking.

for the purpose of eating the sweet red insides at the end of the season. He didn't realize the outside flesh of the gourd was edible until he moved to Hong Kong as a young man and tried stir-fried bitter melon, a popular dish there.

IN THE KITCHEN The outside of the bitter melon flesh is most often cooked in stir-fries or soups. You can tame the bitterness of the melon by slicing and salting prior to cooking, or by blanching the bitter melon in boiling water for a few minutes before using. However, connoisseurs typically opt out of these steps. Bitter melon is usually cooked with hot red peppers or garlic black bean sauce, as the strong flavors balance the bitterness of the melon. To use bitter melon in a stir-fry, slice the gourd in half lengthwise, scoop out and discard the pulp and seeds, then chop into ⅓-inch segments. You'll be left with attractive C-shaped segments to use in your favorite stir-fry. Another method of preparing the bitter melon is to simply cleave off 1-inch hunks of the outer part of the melon and then discard the center that remains.

Bitter melon goes well with the strong tastes of garlic and fermented black beans.

STIR-FRIED BITTER MELON AND TOFU WITH GARLIC AND FERMENTED BLACK BEANS

This dish, served with a small bowl of steamed rice, provides a well-rounded and much-anticipated meal for my vegetarian sister whenever she comes to visit. In a typical stir-fry, bitter melon is cut in half lengthwise, seeded, and sliced into thin C-shaped pieces. In this recipe, I use a different method that results in large pieces of the refreshingly bitter and cooling melon with each bite. To prepare tofu, I like to press the water out by placing the tofu block on a cutting board between towels with a heavy flat object on top. This dries out the tofu, allowing it to soak up the savory, garlicky marinade.

SERVES 4

2 teaspoons garlic, minced

2 teaspoons Shaoxing rice wine

2 teaspoons soy sauce

½ teaspoon dark (toasted) sesame oil

Salt and white pepper

1 block extra firm tofu, pressed for 1 hour and then cut into bite-sized cubes

2 medium (about 8-inch-long) bitter melons

2 tablespoons corn or peanut oil

1 tablespoon fermented black beans, rinsed, drained, and chopped

1. Combine the garlic, rice wine, soy sauce, sesame oil, and salt and pepper to taste in a medium bowl. Add the tofu and marinate for about 1 hour at room temperature, occasionally turning gently.

2. Prepare the bitter melon by cleaving off bite-sized slices of the outer part of the fruit, leaving the pith and seeds behind. It is fine to leave small amounts of white pith on the bitter melon pieces.

3. Heat a wok over medium-high heat until hot, then add the oil. When oil is hot, add the black beans and stir-fry until fragrant, about 10 seconds. Add the bitter melon and stir-fry until almost tender, about 4 minutes. Add tofu along with marinade and cook until tofu cubes are warmed through and just beginning to brown, another 1–2 minutes. Serve immediately with steamed white rice.

Lagenaria siceraria

bottle gourd

MANDARIN *dàjí húlu*
CANTONESE *wu loh gwaa*

大吉葫蘆

葫蘆瓜

Throughout history, bottle gourds have been among the most useful fruits in China. This mild, summer squash–like vegetable is delicious when eaten as a young gourd, but can also serve myriad household uses when allowed to grow the full season and harden. There are many shapes and varieties of gourds in this family, but Chinese gardeners commonly grow a few in particular. The best choice for eating is the elongated, club-shaped gourd generally known as long squash, opo, or calabash. Farmers, families, and artists have used the variety with a bulbous base and very narrow neck, sometimes known as a dipper gourd, for generations. Another popular variety has a double-bulbed or hourglass shape; it can be eaten young, but is usually grown for ornamental purposes.

When bottle gourds are left to mature and dry out, the pale green skin will toughen and harden, and turn a utilitarian khaki color. Then, depending on how the gourds are cut, they can be used for cups, bowls, musical instruments, and birdhouses. My father created a tool that he uses in the garden and as a scoop for duck feed by drying a bottle gourd and then cutting the gourd in half lengthwise. Tied to his rowboat is another large hardened gourd, which he uses to scoop water from the boat when necessary. Whereas wood would rot over time, gourd containers, even when filled with water, will stay watertight and rot-free, sometimes for generations.

Bottle gourds also have numerous health benefits. Eaten in soups, they nourish the lungs, soothe coughs, and contain many vitamins. They are also high in calcium and recommended for older adults to maintain good bone health.

IN THE GARDEN Start bottle gourd plants indoors in early spring. Place two or three seeds about 1½ inches deep in 4-inch pots. When seedlings emerge, thin to leave the strongest one. When the soil in the garden begins to warm in spring, seedlings can be hardened off and then planted in the ground a few feet apart. Alternatively, gardeners with a longer

This variety of bottle gourd, often called long squash, is excellent for eating.

Bottle gourd plants are vigorous and require a structure to climb.

summer season can sow bottle gourds directly in the garden when the soil reaches about 65 degrees Fahrenheit.

Bottle gourds are vigorous vining plants. Strong tendrils help them pull toward the summer sun and each plant will require a structure to climb. If the vine grows too tall, it's possible to cut back long shoots; this does the fruits a favor because they often grow best on lateral shoots, especially the female flowers, which will bear fruit. The bottle gourd is a pretty vine with large leaves and white flowers that open in the evening. If flowers are not producing fruit you may want to

try pollinating by hand to help out the night-flying pollinators. In the evening, when flowers have opened, identify the female flowers by their swollen bases below the bloom that look like tiny bottle gourds (the male flowers usually stand on thinner stems and do not have the tiny fruits under the flower). Rip off a male flower and shake a bit of pollen into the center of the female flower. Each male flower can pollinate several female flowers.

If growing bottle gourds for eating, harvest when the fruits are young and small for their variety. They will

a joyous decoration

When my father does not need bottle gourds for food or products, he may grow another variety with an additional smaller bulb near the top. This double-bulbed type is edible, but not desired for eating because of its awkward shape and small amount of usable flesh. However, these hourglass-shaped gourds are as symbolically auspicious as they are architecturally interesting, and they make for a beautiful decoration around the house. Called *dàjí húlu* in Mandarin, translated to "good luck gourd," (*húlu* meaning bottle gourd), the name is also a synonym for a Chinese phrase that means happiness and prosperity. For decorative purposes, leave gourds to mature on the vine until the end of the season. If they are still not fully hardened, remove from the vine and store in a dry place. When fully dry, my father likes to sand these gourds to perfection. They can then be stained and even lacquered. We hang the gourds with a red string, a color that represents good fortune and joy. Miniature varieties sold as miniature or baby bottle gourds are perfect to give as gifts, for adorning decorations like wreaths, or just to string around the house as good luck charms.

Miniature bottle gourds grown for decorative purposes.

BOTTLE GOURD AND CHICKEN STIR-FRY

This easy stir-fry goes perfectly with a small bowl of rice for a simple meal. When harvested young, the oblong bottle gourd known as long squash is sweet and mild. Other squash such as fuzzy melon or luffa gourd are excellent substitutions for bottle gourd.

SERVES 4–6

- 2 teaspoons light soy sauce
- ½ teaspoon sugar
- 2 teaspoons cornstarch
- 1 teaspoon dark (toasted) sesame oil
- Dash of white pepper
- 1 whole chicken breast, sliced about ⅓ inch thick
- 1–2 bottle gourds (1 pound)
- ½ cup chicken stock or water
- 2–3 tablespoons corn or peanut oil
- ½-inch section of ginger, julienned
- 2 medium yellow onions, thinly sliced
- 1 teaspoon minced garlic
- Pinch of salt

1. Combine the soy sauce, sugar, 1 teaspoon of the cornstarch, sesame oil, and white pepper in a bowl. Add the chicken and marinate for about 30 minutes at room temperature.

2. Peel the bottle gourd with a vegetable peeler. Cut in half and then scoop out and discard the seeds and soft, pithy insides. Cut bottle gourd into bite-sized pieces.

3. Stir the remaining 1 teaspoon cornstarch into the chicken stock. Set aside.

4. Heat a wok over medium-high heat and then add 2 tablespoons of the oil. When hot, add the marinated chicken and stir-fry until cooked through. Remove and set aside.

5. Add another tablespoon of oil to the wok if necessary. When hot, add the ginger and cook, stirring, until fragrant, about 30 seconds. Add the onions, then cover and cook, stirring occasionally for about 2 minutes. Add the bottle gourd and continue to cook for another 5 minutes, stirring occasionally. Add the minced garlic and salt and cook until the gourd and onions are tender, about 15 minutes. Finally, add the cooked chicken and cornstarch solution. When sauce bubbles and thickens, remove from heat and serve with steamed white rice.

be firm, with a shiny light green skin. The gourds will become bitter, and then tough, fibrous, and inedible, as they mature. Long squash, the elongated type that is preferable for eating, is not only larger but can be allowed to grow closer to maturity than the bulbous-bottomed types. Bottle gourds are ready for eating in about 60 days. To grow for household or crafting purposes, gourds require about 100 days to maturity.

IN THE KITCHEN Young bottle gourd is mild and has a pleasant, soft texture similar to other Chinese summer squash. Some compare it to a cucumber, but with a lower water content. Peel the club-shaped long squash before using. If harvested young, you can eat the pith and immature seeds, but most people choose to discard any spongy insides along with the seeds. Preparations for bottle gourd include braising, stir-frying, baking, or cooking in soups. To prevent nutrient loss, do not overcook. Bottle gourds complement most dishes and will work well in any recipe that calls for zucchini or other summer squash.

To use the type with a single large bulbous base for culinary purposes, prepare and cook it in the same way as long squash. To use these gourds for household or craft purposes, simply allow them to dry on the vine. Alternatively, you can prepare the gourd in a way to both preserve the shell and use the flesh. Near the end of the summer when the gourds are ripe but not yet dry, cut the gourd in half lengthwise. Remove the pith and seeds and then steam the halves for about 30 minutes until the flesh is soft and cooked (steaming keeps the shell from collapsing as it dries). At that point, you can remove the flesh and allow the shell to dry fully to become hardened and watertight. After removing the flesh, you can either cook it as desired or dehydrate it for use later. My father describes the rehydrated bottle gourd flesh as almost meaty like chicken breast. Slice or cut it into pieces and use it like a fleshy mushroom or protein.

Allium fistulosum

bunching onions

MANDARIN *dàcōng, xiǎocōng*
CANTONESE *dai tsung, siu tsung*

大
葱

小
葱

Bunching onions have been grown in China for centuries. You can always find space for this slim-profiled, shallow-rooted plant, whether in its own plot in the vegetable garden, in an ornamental bed, or in any well-draining container with a few inches of rich soil. Bunching onions are less fussy than bulb onions, which require a longer growing period, and which leave an empty hole in the garden once harvested. In contrast, bunching onions do not form a bulb, but grow prolifically throughout the season.

In the kitchen, bunching onions provide a strong, but not overpowering, oniony-garlicky flavor. They're a great addition to most any recipe and are nutritious as well. The next time you make chicken soup to ease a cold, add a generous amount of these onions. They help boost the immune system and contain vitamins A, B, and C, iron, and calcium.

IN THE GARDEN Multi-stemmed bunching onions are a hardy perennial and increase every year; 'Evergreen' or 'Four Seasons' are good varieties to try. In cold climates in China, people sometimes cut onions from under snow cover. For summer harvesting, sow seed ¼–½ inch deep directly in the garden in the spring, or start indoors and transplant, spacing 2–6 inches apart. Heat will speed germination. Plant single-stemmed types, such as the Japanese 'Shimonita Negi', closer together, but give multi-stemmed types more room to increase in size. For fall or early spring harvesting, sow seed directly in the garden in late summer. Cut and eat bunching onions as young shoots, or wait until they reach their typical height at maturity of about 18 inches. Bunching onions are easy to grow, resistant to pests and diseases—just keep the garden bed relatively weed-free.

Gardeners who want to cultivate a long blanched stem for a more tender onion should transplant onions into trenches about 12 inches deep. When the stems are about 3 inches tall, fill in the trench to cover most of

Mid-summer onion blooms atop
Chinese bunching onions.

dàcōng

Dàcōng in Mandarin, meaning "big onion," is a unique variety of single-stemmed bunching onion grown as an annual. To grow this very tall onion, plant it in in a trench and then hill it up as it grows throughout the summer to produce a tender white section almost 2 feet from the root. My parents sometimes dip this extremely tender and mildly pungent onion in plum sauce and just take big bites out of it. Another benefit of *dàcōng* is its ability to store well. In Shandong, before a hard frost, the onions are all dug out of the garden, five or six are braided together, and then they are stored upright in a tall ceramic pot in a cold room of the house. The coveted white section of the onion loses most of its bite, resulting in a tender vegetable with a sweet onion flavor.

Dàcōng, a leek-like variety of bunching onion, is hilled up as it grows, creating a tender onion that is eaten as a vegetable.

Bunching onions are easy to grow but they don't compete well with weeds.

You can use large Chinese bunching onions like you would scallions or green onions.

the stem with rich, well-draining soil, leaving the top above the soil line. Earthing up the stem like this blanches it, keeping it tender. Single-stemmed bunching onions look almost like leeks and can grow just as thick and tall. Single-stemmed varieties are tender and mild when grown using this method.

Onions will eventually flower, which can reduce the quality of taste, but you can still eat them. Some gardeners will grow successive crops in order to have tender onions throughout the season. Multi-stemmed onions will divide and send up other shoots. To harvest, cut off what is needed, or carefully pull off a division.

IN THE KITCHEN In my family, we use chopped onions as a garnish for stir-fries, thinly sliced to top noodles and noodle soup dishes, cut into lengths for braising, crushed into sauces, and in a plethora of other ways. The onion flavor can be delicate or more pungent, depending on the season of harvest, amount used, and method of cooking. If you have not yet tried bunching onions, I encourage you to give this go-with-everything, easy-to-grow vegetable a chance. Experiment by using them in most Asian food recipes or whenever you have a need for the pungent flavor of leek, chive, garlic, shallot, or onion.

ANISE CHICKEN WITH CRUSHED GINGER AND ONION DIPPING OIL

This is one of my favorite dishes that my mom makes. The slow cooking produces an incredibly tender, moist, and subtly flavored chicken. In this variation of a Hainanese-style recipe, a condiment made by pouring hot oil over crushed ginger and onion brings out the aromatic flavors. I love a dinner of steamed white rice, several slices of the tender anise-scented chicken, and a generous spoonful of the delicious ginger and onion oil. The simple sauce comes together quickly, but to follow the full recipe, factor in an extra 1–3 days prior to cooking in order to infuse the chicken with anise flavor.

SERVES 4-6

1 (3-pound) whole chicken

2 tablespoons plus 1 teaspoon salt

20 pieces whole star anise

2-inch section of ginger, peeled and sliced

3 bunching onions, cut into 2-inch lengths

¼ cup corn or peanut oil

1. Rinse the chicken, pat dry, and rub inside and out with the 2 tablespoons salt. Add the star anise to the inside of the chicken. Cover or seal in a brining bag and refrigerate for 1–3 days.

2. Remove the chicken from the refrigerator and set out for 1 hour to allow it to come to room temperature.

3. Add enough water to a stock pot so that the chicken will be completely covered when added. Bring water to a boil. When the water is boiling, carefully lower the chicken, along with the star anise, into the pot. Allow the water to come back up to a boil and then reduce heat to medium low. Simmer chicken uncovered for 10 minutes. Skim off any residue from top of water. Turn off heat. Immediately cover with tight-fitting lid and allow to steep undisturbed for another 45 minutes until chicken is cooked through. While chicken is steeping, make the ginger and onion oil.

4. To make the ginger and onion oil: crush ginger and bunching onions with a mortar and pestle or smash on a cutting board with a rolling pin. (You could also chop by hand or pulse in a food processor, but crushing with mortar and pestle provides a more traditional taste and texture.) Place the ginger and onions in a heatproof bowl and add the 1 teaspoon salt.

5. Heat the oil until hot but not smoking in a saucepan. Slowly pour the hot oil onto the ginger and onion mixture. Be careful as hot oil may splatter.

6. When chicken is cooked through, remove carefully from the pot. Reserve the cooking liquid to make the rice, or save for another use. Lower the chicken into an ice water bath to quickly stop the process of cooking. In about 15 minutes, when chicken is cool, remove from ice water bath, pat dry and chop into pieces. Serve with the ginger and onion oil over steamed white rice.

Cucumis sativus

chinese cucumbers

MANDARIN *huángguā*
CANTONESE *wong gwaa*

黄
瓜

It's no wonder that Chinese cucumbers are making their way into more and more backyard gardens. Chinese cucumbers taste similar to the cucumbers that most of us are familiar with, but many people find them sweeter and crisper. They also tend to have fewer seeds and are more easily digestible. In fact, many gardeners may already be growing Chinese cucumbers without even knowing it. Any cucumber that is long, slender, and labeled "burpless" has a good chance of being a Chinese cucumber; 'Tokiwa' and 'Suyo Long' are excellent cultivars to try.

Chinese medicine practitioners may recommend making cucumbers a regular part of the diet to thin the blood. The thirst-quenching juice is also known for contributing to a bright complexion and smooth skin. When my sister got locked out of the house as a kid, she would pluck cucumbers from the garden, wipe them off with her sleeve, and successfully stave off afterschool hunger until my mom returned home.

IN THE GARDEN Chinese cucumbers are a sight in the garden as they can grow to about 3 feet long with slight ridges and prickly skin. They are easy to grow and have the same growing requirements as American cucumbers. Some people choose to start seeds indoors, whereas others prefer to sow directly in the garden. I've found that when seeds are sown in the late spring, after the soil begins to warm, the vines quickly catch up to seedlings started indoors. To start outdoors, sow seeds about 1 inch deep and 6 inches apart. As the seedlings grow, thin to 12–24 inches apart. Although you can allow cucumbers to ramble on the ground, a fence or trellis will accommodate the vigorous vine and help the cucumbers grow straight. Training the vine up a trellis also leaves more room in the garden for other plants.

During the growing season, keep the vines well watered for sweet and juicy cucumbers. If your cucumbers

Chinese cucumbers are sweeter, crisper, and have fewer seeds than their Western counterparts.

Cool Chinese cucumbers are delicious when marinated in black vinegar, sesame oil, spicy peppercorn oil, and other ingredients.

taste bitter, try watering more deeply and frequently. On hot summer days, it is not uncommon for leaves to look wilted, but they should liven up again in the cooler mornings. Harvest Chinese cucumbers at any stage of growing as soon as they've filled out a bit. It's important to stay on top of harvesting because cucumbers left to mature will signal the vine to stop producing. Keep picking to keep the vine productive.

IN THE KITCHEN Sweet, crisp, and juicy, Chinese cucumbers are refreshing when eaten raw in salads and as pickles. Chinese cooks love to pair cool cucumbers with some spice as well. One snack I look forward to every summer is my mom's marinated cucumbers made with spicy Sichuan peppercorns, sesame oil, and lots of garlic. The cool and crisp cucumbers in a hot garlicky sauce are addictive. You can also sauté or stir-fry cucumbers, using any recipe that calls for summer squash, or use cucumbers in soups. Salting prepares the cucumbers for cooking by removing the excess water that would hinder the stir-fry process.

SPICY SICHUAN PEPPERCORN–MARINATED CUCUMBERS

Sichuan peppercorns (*huā jiāo*) have a complex flavor and create a numbing sensation in the mouth. In this and other pickle recipes, I prefer Chinese cucumbers to their Western counterparts because they are crisper and contain fewer seeds. When making this dish, or any other pickle, I recommend sweating the cucumbers first to draw out excess moisture, ensuring that a watery cucumber does not dilute the marinade or pickling liquid.

MAKES ABOUT A QUART OF PICKLES

2–3 long Chinese cucumbers

1 tablespoon salt

½ teaspoon Sichuan peppercorns

1 teaspoon hot chile paste

2 teaspoons dark (toasted) sesame oil

1 teaspoon sugar

1 teaspoon Chinkiang or another black vinegar like balsamic

1 large clove garlic, very thinly sliced

1. Prepare the cucumbers by cutting each into 4-inch sections. Cut each section into six spears. Place the cucumbers in a colander in the sink and sprinkle with salt. Mix and allow to sit for an hour. Pat dry with a kitchen towel or paper towel and then pack loosely in a glass jar.

2. Combine the peppercorns, chile paste, sesame oil, sugar, vinegar, and garlic in a small bowl and then pour the mixture over the cucumber spears. Refrigerate for at least 2 hours.

My mom's spicy quick pickle made with garlic and Sichuan peppercorns.

Solanum melongena

chinese eggplants

MANDARIN *qiézi*
CANTONESE *ke zi*

茄
子

Eggplants grown in Asia vary in appearance ranging from the firm, pea-sized eggplant, to the green, apricot-sized Thai eggplant, to a tart orange eggplant. Despite an abundance of shapes and sizes grown around the world, many cooks of varied ethnic backgrounds prefer the long and slender Asian eggplants, often known as Chinese or Japanese eggplants. Chinese eggplants are paler in color and have a milder flavor in contrast to the slightly bitter, deep purple globe eggplants typically found in the West. Our family prefers Chinese eggplants because they usually contain fewer seeds and have thinner skins. 'Ping Tung' is a delicious variety that is productive in the garden and has a mild, sweet taste.

With their intricate purple flowers, eggplants are sometimes grown primarily for their blooms. They're stunning when grown in rows in the garden as well as in ornamental pots with contrasting annual flowering plants. Eggplants also offer many health benefits in traditional Chinese medicine. They are known to lower cholesterol and blood pressure and are also good for general eye health.

IN THE GARDEN To reap plentiful harvests of Chinese eggplant, start seeds indoors 6–8 weeks before your last spring frost. Soaking the seed overnight and providing heat will help speed up the slow germination process. Move eggplant seedlings outdoors to a sunny spot after the soil has warmed to about 60 degrees Fahrenheit. Tiny pests such as flea beetles love to nibble pinholes in the leaves; if this has been a problem in your garden in past years, take preventative measures by using a floating row cover or planting in containers up off the ground. Diatomaceous earth is also effective against flea beetles. Because flea beetles are known to be able to pick up the scent of eggplant, planting fragrant herbs and other companion plants (such as marigolds, catnip, thyme, dill, and mint) near eggplant may help hide the plants from persistent garden pests. This may also attract beneficial insects, an added bonus.

Chinese eggplants are as versatile in the kitchen as they are beautiful.

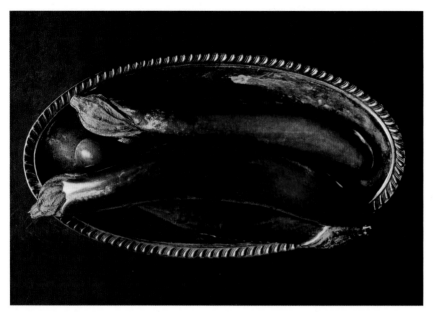

Long and thin, Chinese eggplants contain fewer seeds and have thinner skins than globe eggplants.

Chinese eggplants are heavy producers, so the plants should be staked before they get too heavy with fruit. Once the plant starts fruiting, eggplants can be picked for a long season. They are ready to be harvested when they have developed a bright purple color, have a glossy skin, and when they are still firm, but no longer hard. When you press a finger on the eggplant, you should be able to gently indent it, but the flesh should bounce back. An eggplant that is dull or does not bounce back after pressing is past its prime and will often taste bitter.

IN THE KITCHEN Eggplant's versatility makes it a welcome addition to just about any dish. Many cooks enjoy Chinese eggplants for their mild taste, which pairs well with the strong flavors of garlic or spices, and thin, tender skins that do not need to be peeled. And unlike many other varieties of eggplant, Chinese eggplants don't require salting before cooking. In China, eggplants are sliced, diced, mashed, steamed, boiled, or deep-fried. Though they can be stir-fried as well, eggplants are often battered and fried instead because they tend to soak up liquids and can quickly become soggy with oil if fried directly.

STEAMED EGGPLANT WITH GARLIC SESAME SAUCE

This is a small plate dish that is unbelievable in its simplicity. When my mom finishes this easy dish and reenters the kitchen to continue cooking, we tend to converge around the table sneaking bites. One time, the plate was near empty before the rest of dinner was ready.

SERVES 4 AS A SIDE DISH

2 Chinese eggplants

1 teaspoon minced garlic

½ teaspoon dark (toasted) sesame oil

3 tablespoons light soy sauce

1 tablespoon rice wine vinegar

1. In a tall stockpot, set the whole eggplants in a steamer basket. Add about an inch of water to the pot. Bring to a boil and then cover and steam until tender, about 15 minutes. Cut each eggplant in half lengthwise and place on serving plate. Lightly cut or tear the eggplant apart. The goal is not to mash the eggplant, but just to tear it a bit so it's able to hold the delicious sauce.

2. Combine the garlic, sesame oil, soy sauce, and vinegar in a small bowl. Pour the sauce over the eggplant and serve warm or at room temperature.

Capsicum annuum

chinese peppers

MANDARIN *làjiāo*
CANTONESE *laat ziu*

辣
椒

The Chinese provinces of Hunan, Sichuan, and Yunnan are known for their hot foods. 'Tien Tsin' chile peppers are a well-known variety of red chile pepper grown in China. These fiery and pungent peppers come from Tientsin, China, and are used to add heat in Hunan and Sichuan cuisines. It is often the variety dried and added to spicy restaurant dishes such as kung pao chicken. Resembling a mini cayenne pepper at 1½ inches long, these red chile peppers are incredibly hot. They score about 60,000 Scoville heat units (in contrast, a jalapeno scores about 2,500–8,000 Scoville heat units).

'Facing Heaven' is another Chinese pepper variety to try. It is stockier (about 1½ inches long with a wide base) and less hot than 'Tien Tsin'. This medium-hot pepper has a thin skin and is also often used whole to add a spicy flavor to Sichuan dishes.

Aside from contributing to the strong flavor profile of regional foods, hot peppers stimulate the appetite, warm the body, and aid in weight loss too. Chinese hot peppers are all high in vitamins A, B, and C, as well as iron and calcium.

IN THE GARDEN Peppers are tender perennials, but are typically grown as warm-weather annuals. Start seeds indoors in early spring. It may take 1–2 weeks for pepper seeds to germinate and a little heat will hasten germination. Raise seedlings under a grow light or by a bright window for the next several weeks. When the soil in the garden warms to 60-65 degrees Fahrenheit, harden seedlings off and transplant to a sunny spot in the garden. Space plants about 12 inches apart and water deeply as needed. 'Tien Tsin', 'Facing Heaven', and many other varieties of Chinese peppers, will grow pointing up and will turn red as they ripen. Peppers will be ready for harvesting in 80–100 days.

Peppers are relatively free of pests, although I've caught hornworms chewing them from time to time.

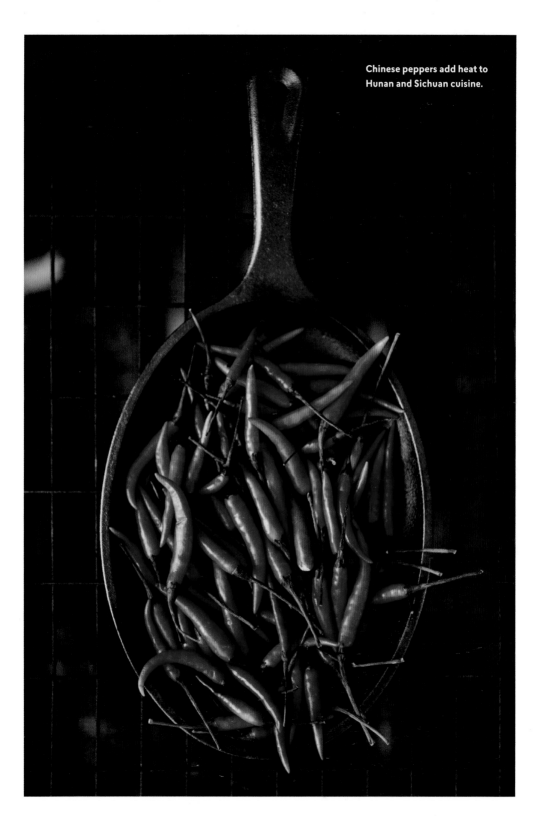

Chinese peppers add heat to Hunan and Sichuan cuisine.

Keep an eye out: if left undiscovered, a hornworm can quickly decimate a pepper plant.

IN THE KITCHEN Chinese peppers such as 'Tien Tsin' are extremely hot, and like most peppers, the heat is located in the membranes that the seeds are attached to inside the pepper. For this reason, these peppers are often added whole in dishes and then removed before serving. If I will be chopping first, I like to have the aromatic flavor and some spice of the pepper without unbearable heat, so I will sometimes double the peppers, but remove most of what's inside before chopping and cooking. Plants often produce much more than can be used, so it's smart to save peppers by drying them in the sun, a dehydrator, or oven, or even by vacuum sealing and freezing.

An excellent use for Chinese peppers is for making hot chile sauce, or simply adding heat to some oil in the wok before stir-frying a dish. Another idea is to heat up some sesame oil, add a handful of dried peppers, and fry until lightly browned and fragrant. Let the mixture cool and then add it to a half a cup of peanut oil. This creates a flavorful oil that you can use as a base for a spicy sauce or for stir-frying.

Spicy and decadent, XO sauce makes good use of a glut of summer peppers.

XO SAUCE

Created in Hong Kong, the name of this coveted sauce—a reference to the extra-old ("XO") cognac enjoyed by the Hong Kong elite—hints at the decadent and classy ingredients it contains. I love this slightly spicy savory sauce on just about anything, but especially mixed into a bowl of fresh noodles. My husband loves it on dumplings, and it is also an excellent condiment to serve alongside steamed white rice and other stir-fry dishes. My mom has crafted a vegetarian version for my sister by substituting peanuts and cashews for the dried seafood. This recipe is easy but somewhat time-consuming because of the soaking required for the scallops and shrimp; consider doubling and freezing it—you'll be happy you did.

MAKES ABOUT 2 CUPS

½ cup dried scallops

½ cup dried shrimp

½ cup garlic cloves, peeled

½ cup fresh ginger, peeled and sliced

2 shallots, sliced

2 fresh, long, red Chinese peppers, seeded and chopped

1 cup country ham, chopped

1 cup canola or corn oil

1 tablespoon dried red pepper flakes

Pinch of sugar

Salt

1. Place the dried scallops and dried shrimp in a medium bowl and add water to cover by an inch. Allow to soak for 4–8 hours, until completely soft.

2. Put the garlic, ginger, shallots, and Chinese peppers in a food processor and pulse until finely minced. The aim is to have finely minced ingredients, not to create a paste. Empty the contents into a bowl. Drain the scallops and shrimp, and pulse in food processor until finely minced. Place in the bowl with the garlic mixture.

3. Add the ham to the food processor and pulse until finely minced. Heat the oil over medium-high heat in a skillet. When hot, add the ham and stir occasionally until it begins to crisp, 2–3 minutes. Add the red pepper flakes and stir. Reduce heat to medium-low and add remaining minced ingredients to pan. Cook for about 30 minutes, or until the ingredients take on a uniform deep golden brown color. Remove from the heat and add a pinch of sugar and salt to taste. When cool, store in a jar in the refrigerator. It will last for about a month.

Hemerocallis fulva

daylily buds

金
針

MANDARIN *jīnzhēn*
CANTONESE *gum zum*

The cheerful daylily is a cornerstone in many perennial gardens. Its profusion of blooms, bright color, and ease of care are attractive to gardeners. But what many gardeners don't know is that the daylily is a delicacy enjoyed in Chinese dishes. The unopened buds have a sweet taste and a crisp, sort of al dente texture that is almost squeaky between the teeth, described in one word as *song* in Cantonese. Daylily buds are excellent raw in salads, or cooked in stir-fries, soups, and noodle dishes. Daylily buds are also called *mong yao cho* in Cantonese, meaning "a grass that makes one forget about worries." This is due to their antidepressant and energizing qualities.

IN THE GARDEN If you're not already growing daylilies, you probably know someone who is. Because the plants naturalize freely, it's likely that your friend or neighbor won't mind dividing and sharing with you. If you need to buy your own, choose the original common yellow or orange daylily, *Hemerocallis fulva*. My parents grow a delicious yellow Chinese field crop type passed along from friend to friend. If you can't get your hands on a variety known to taste great, look for the plain, orange lilies commonly found in the wild, in masses in your friend's backyard, near roadsides, sunny fields, and even in ditches (hence their nickname—ditch lilies).

These have a slightly bitter but still sweet flavor. Avoid daylily cultivars that may be beautiful but are not proven edible.

Daylilies have fleshy tuberous roots, and divisions should be set at the same level they were growing at previously, with the crown just below the soil level. Space plants 12–24 inches apart. Daylilies are easy to care for as well as easy to move. Beyond appreciating compost dug into the planting hole, they are not too particular.

The best time to plant daylilies depends on your region. In the northern parts of North America, spring is a good time to plant so plants have

Daylily blooms brighten up spring gardens and the buds are sweet and delicious to eat.

deterring deer

As much as I enjoy the beauty of daylilies and the food my mom makes with the unopened buds, so do the deer that live in my neighborhood. I regularly spray the different varieties of lilies, hosta, and phlox in my perennial garden to keep the deer away. If I am consistent, they leave all my plants alone. The best products I've tried are chemical-free, but are still generally made with the urine of various animals. I obviously don't want to treat my edible buds with these products and instead rely on other tricks to keep the deer away, such as situating my daylilies behind hellebores and other plants that deer generally avoid. My father grows a beautiful mass of daylilies just inside his tall garden fence. This must drive the deer crazy.

a few frost-free (or at least frost-unlikely) months to establish their roots. In the South, a cooler time of year is best, as opposed to the hot and humid summer months when plants may either rot or dry up before having a chance to establish themselves. Water regularly after planting until established. They'll quickly become accustomed to just about any soil and are hardy in most of North America. Like most perennials, the size of the plant and the number of blooms will increase in the first few years.

Daylilies are aptly named: although the plants appear vibrant, with blooms that seem to last for weeks, each flower lasts for only one day. It is simply the sheer number of blooms that gives the impression of being so long lasting. For eating, pick buds in the morning when plump and just before they open. Because daylilies produce blooms for a long season, buds will be available for picking whenever the cook needs them.

IN THE KITCHEN To prepare daylily buds for eating, gently squeeze the tip of the bud open and pinch off the pollen-covered anthers. Before cooking, soak and rinse carefully to remove any hidden insects or dirt. You can also harvest and air-dry daylily buds for use after the flowering period. To rehydrate dried flower buds before cooking, soak in cool water until soft, about an hour.

To capture the best daylily buds for eating, pick when they are plump, in the morning just before they open.

You can rehydrate dried daylily buds and then use them in a stir-fry or noodle dish.

DAI LO MEIN

This Northern Chinese noodle soup dish is the epitome of comfort food. A good Chinese host will always insist on refilling your bowl—even if you're not nearly close to being done. I love how just a small handful of daylily buds adds contrasting texture, flavor, and bright color to this noodle soup dish. This recipe includes several dried ingredients that require soaking ahead of time, so plan accordingly.

SERVES 6

¼ cup cornstarch

6 cups chicken stock

¼ cup dried shrimp, soaked in water until soft, about 4 hours

4 slices of ginger, ¼ inch thick

3 green onions, cut into 2-inch segments

½ pound pork belly, cooked and then thinly sliced

2 tablespoons corn or peanut oil

4 dried shiitake mushrooms, soaked in warm water until soft, about 1 hour, then cut into thick chunks

6 pieces dried wood ear, soaked in warm water until soft, about 1 hour

2 eggs

1 cup fresh daylily buds

About ¾ pound dried white wheat noodles

⅓ cup coarsely chopped cilantro for garnish

1. Stir cornstarch into 1 cup of the chicken broth. Set aside.

2. Heat a large stockpot over high heat and then add the oil. When hot, add the shrimp, ginger, green onions, and pork belly. Stir-fry until fragrant, 1–2 minutes.

3. Add the remaining 5 cups chicken stock, mushrooms, and wood ear to the pot. Bring to a boil and simmer for 10 minutes. Add the cornstarch solution to the pot and bring to a boil again.

4. Lightly beat the eggs in a small bowl. Slowly add to the soup, stirring once. Stir in the daylily buds and turn off the heat.

5. Cook and drain the noodles according to package directions. Serve the soup over the noodles and garnish generously with cilantro.

edible lily bulbs

Another edible flower delicacy in Chinese cuisine is called *baah hop* in Cantonese (*bǎi hé* in Mandarin) or lily bulb. Although many species of lily bulbs are edible, *Lilium brownii* is most commonly used in Chinese cooking. Its large trumpet-shaped blooms are beautiful, but it's the edible bulbs under the ground that Chinese cooks go for. The bulbs, pristine and white on the inside, are made of thick petal-like sections that are pulled apart and cooked in savory stir-fries and soups. My favorite way to eat lily bulb is in a warm, sweet soup that my mom sometimes makes when we are sick. Lily bulbs are used in traditional Chinese medicine and are known for improving coughs, soothing the lungs, and reducing symptoms of asthma. You can find lily bulbs prepared for eating in Asian supermarkets.

Benincasa hispida var. *chieh-qua*

fuzzy melon

MANDARIN *máoguā*
CANTONESE *zeet gwaa*

毛瓜

節瓜

Pleasant tasting, firm-textured, and versatile, this summer vegetable deserves a place in every garden and kitchen. Covered with fine soft hairs, fuzzy melon is sometimes called hairy melon. Some people compare fuzzy melon to the Chinese winter melon and find it is similar in its texture and mild taste, but with a size that can be easier to work with. Any dish that calls for zucchini or yellow squash would also work well with fuzzy melon. In the garden, this vine likes a structure to climb, saving valuable space on the ground for other vegetables. Fuzzy melon is known for its medicinal ability to clear toxins and cool the body. It is also loaded with vitamin C and other nutrients. The popular 'Seven Star Long' has a classic size, shape, and taste, and is a good choice for growing at home.

IN THE GARDEN Start fuzzy melons outside after the soil has warmed to about 65 degrees Fahrenheit. Plant two or three seeds 1 inch deep in each planting hole spaced about 12 inches apart. When seedlings emerge, thin to leave the strongest one standing. You'll need to provide a trellis, pole, or fence to stake the vine, allowing the fruits to hang down as they grow. With regular watering and full sun, the prolific fuzzy melon plant will produce numerous plump, vaguely pear-shaped gourds. As with zucchini, picking young fruits will ensure the best taste and texture. A young fuzzy melon will be small and firm with thin, beautifully blotchy, bright green skin. Harvest fuzzy melons when they are 6–8 inches long and covered with soft, downy hairs.

IN THE KITCHEN To prepare fuzzy melon, simply remove the soft fuzz covering the squash by scraping the outside of the melon with the back of a knife. They don't need to be peeled, and in fact, like most vegetables, much of the nutrition is in the skin. If harvested early, fuzzy melon seeds will be white, very small, and edible. If harvested later, you may need to seed

Fuzzy melon is versatile in the kitchen—use it in any recipe that calls for squash or zucchini.

the melon before using. The seeded melon can then be cut into slices, dice, chunks, or matchsticks. For a more interesting presentation, cut the melon in half lengthwise, scoop out the seeds with a spoon, stuff it with a filling, and steam it. The mildly sweet taste and great smooth texture go well with just about any meat, vegetable, or sauce. To create a visually appealing dish, try cooking fuzzy melon with foods of contrasting colors such as bright orange carrots or black mushrooms.

SAUTÉED FUZZY MELON

Sometimes the best way to enjoy a vegetable is by itself—unclouded by heavy sauces, and without competition from other vegetables or ingredients. Fuzzy melon shines in this simple preparation.

SERVES 4 AS A SIDE DISH

1 (1½-pound) fuzzy melon

2 tablespoons corn or peanut oil

Sea salt

1. Using the back of a chef's knife, scrape the fine hairs off the fuzzy melon. Rinse and pat dry. Cut into round slices about ¾ inch thick.

2. In a skillet over medium heat, add the oil. When hot, work in batches and carefully add enough slices of melon to cover the pan. Cook until golden, about 2 minutes per side. Fuzzy melon is finished when just tender. Sprinkle with sea salt to taste.

Vigna unguiculata subsp. *sesquipedalis*

long beans

MANDARIN *lóngdòu*
CANTONESE *cheung gong dao*

龍豆 長江豆

When I was young, the back of my uncle's summer garden was a magical place. There, tall bamboo stakes holding up a makeshift arbor supported vigorous leafy vines where fantastically long green beans hung down two by two. Up close you could see the pretty pale lavender flowers. Chinese long beans, a relative of the cow pea, are a favorite of my children who love the asparagus-like taste. I don't even have to sell them on the fact that fiber-rich long beans are known to have high levels of folates, vitamin C, and other vitamins and minerals. In the garden, long beans are also fun to grow because during the hot summer months one can practically measure new growth each day. The several varieties of long beans are categorized by the red, black, or white color of the mature seeds. One particularly beautiful variety is 'Red Noodle', a long purple-red bean. This bean is stunning in the garden and turns green when cooked.

IN THE GARDEN Long beans thrive in the heat of summer and require a relatively short season, about 60 days, to produce edible pods. Once the soil has completely warmed to about 70 degrees Fahrenheit, plant seeds directly in the garden about ½ inch deep and 6 inches apart. Seeds germinate quickly in a week or so, and in hot weather the vine will quickly take off and grow to more than 10 feet in height. Chinese long beans are a pole bean. In milder zones, twine may be enough to support the plant; gardeners in warmer climates, where plants may grow more vigorously, should provide a sturdier support structure.

Long beans have been known to grow to 3 feet. However, for best taste, harvest when they're around 12 inches long and still slender, young, and crisp. If left on the vine too long, they will be too tough to enjoy. Toward the middle of the summer, you may need to check and harvest long beans daily. Long beans, like other green beans, grow quickly and must be picked regularly in order to remain productive.

Cut long beans into shorter lengths before cooking. They hold up well in stir-fries and against strong tastes like garlic and spice.

IN THE KITCHEN Cooks love the stringless Chinese long bean with its crisp texture and mild flavor. With a vigorous crop of long beans that are cut into 2- to 3-inch lengths, it's possible to try a lot of different recipes each summer. Many restaurants deep-fry long beans to preserve the sweetness and capture the gorgeous bright green color. To deep-fry, add beans to oil in small batches and cook for a few minutes until beans start to shrivel slightly. This shriveling describes the name of a popular restaurant green bean dish, "wrinkled man bean."

Long beans are heartier and studier than a typical Western green bean, making them a great foil for stronger flavors and spice. They're ideal stir-fried because they stand up to being tossed around over a high heat. For a simpler everyday side dish, stir-fry beans using garlic, shallots, or any seasonings you like. Long beans that are lighter in color often have a softer texture more conducive to blanching or quick cooking, whereas darker long beans are generally firmer and thus better for stir-fries or braising, or for dishes that require a longer cooking time or higher heat.

LONG BEANS WITH GARLIC AND PRESERVED OLIVES

Chinese "olives," which can be found in Asian supermarkets, are similar only in appearance to Mediterranean olives. The taste of these fruits resembles a sour or preserved plum, with a slightly sweet fragrance and a hint of five-spice powder. They're often sold packed in clear pouches labeled as salted olives or preserved olives. If you can't find this unique ingredient, simply cook this dish with garlic alone or with garlic and about 1 tablespoon of rinsed and chopped fermented black beans. (If using fermented black beans, limit or omit the soy sauce, as the fermented black beans are salty.)

SERVES 4 AS A SIDE DISH

2 tablespoons corn or peanut oil

1 pound Chinese long beans, cut into 2- to 3-inch lengths

4 Chinese preserved olives, finely chopped

4 large garlic cloves, chopped

⅓ cup water

Soy sauce for serving

Pinch of sugar

1. Heat oil in a wok over high heat. When hot, add the beans and stir-fry until slightly wrinkled, 5–8 minutes. Add the olives and garlic and continue to stir-fry.

2. After another minute or two, when the garlic begins to turn golden, add the water and cover, stirring occasionally. Continue to steam beans for another few minutes. When crisp-tender, and just before removing from heat, add a drizzle of soy sauce and a pinch of sugar. Stir and serve.

Nelumbo nucifera

lotus

MANDARIN *lien ŏu*
CANTONESE *leen ngau*

蓮藕

My father's summer landscape is a classic scene from a Chinese painting. White geese amble across a wooden footbridge over a stream. In the background, weeping willows edge the pond and sway with any slight breeze. Floating on the surface of the water are large flat lotus leaves, which set off tall, sublime, white blooms. The lotus is a well-known symbol of the past, present, and future: visible on the plant at the same time are the seedpods, huge open blooms, as well as swollen round buds with no intention of unfurling just quite yet. The lotus flower is also a symbol of purity as the large, immaculate white flowers arise from plantings from the bottom of the pond. The pristine blooms seem to appear wondrously from the water.

Lotus plants have numerous uses besides being beautiful. You can harvest the seeds or "nuts" from the seedpods during the summer and eat them as a snack. Some of my older Malaysian friends have told me stories about going to

A pink-flowering variety of lotus opens in the morning among tall seedpods.

Lotus seeds are edible, and the dried seedpods are interesting elements in a floral arrangement.

The rhizome of the lotus plant is easily recognizable by the pattern of holes that show up when sliced.

the movies and buying lotus seedpods atop tall stems from street vendors. As children, they not only enjoyed plucking out the lotus seeds to snack on, but also used to run around with thin pieces of triangular-shaped seed coverings stuck on their fingertips, as if monsters from the films they'd just watched.

Good sources of protein and minerals, lotus seeds are also a general nutritive and restorative in traditional Chinese medicine. Lotus seed paste, commonly found in Chinese pastries, is delicious when slightly sweetened. Lotus root is a good source of fiber and vitamin C and contains healthful phytonutrients that help prevent disease. The young stems and flowers of the lotus plant are also edible, and all parts are used in different cultures in Asia.

The long, segmented rhizomes of the plant, commonly known as lotus root (but not technically a root), are a delicacy in Chinese cuisine. When sliced, each round disk contains a fascinating pattern of holes due to the long air channels that run the length of the rhizome.

IN THE GARDEN Lotus plants are fairly easy to grow for ornamental purposes. One needs only full sun and a pond to accommodate this water plant. Lotuses are perennial plants hardy in zones 5–10. Although you can start them from seed, this is a slower and less reliable process than getting a rhizome from a friend or a mail-order company. In spring, after last frost, plant lotus rhizomes horizontally about 2 inches deep, with new growing tips pointing up from the surface of the soil. The base of the rhizome can slant downward slightly. The waterline should be 6–12 inches above the soil line.

If you don't have a pond, you can grow lotus plants in a large container, at least 3–4 feet in diameter. One lotus root can grow to a few feet long and may curve or bend to take the shape of the container. To grow in a container, fill with a sandy potting soil mix, plant as you would in the ground, and flood with water. Water should be sun-warmed if possible; although cold tolerant, new plants may become stressed if thrust into cold water. Lotuses need about 90 days of soil temperatures between 75 and 87 degrees Fahrenheit in order to bloom.

Clay soils may be too dense to allow any harvestable rhizomes to form. In China, special planting ponds are designated for growing plump lotus rhizomes for eating. The soil in these beds is typically a soft mud and sand mixture. To harvest the rhizomes, wait until the end of the season in mid-fall and carefully dig. The rhizomes will be segmented and will look almost like a short string of giant sausages. Take what you need but be sure to save some segments to be replanted.

Lotuses will overwinter as long as the rhizomes do not freeze. In very cold climates or in shallow ponds that freeze solid over the winter, dig up the rhizomes, bury them in a bucket of damp sand, and store in a cool area so the plant remains dormant. Check on the lotus rhizome periodically to be sure the sand hasn't dried out.

IN THE KITCHEN The rhizome or root is the most commonly eaten part of this completely edible plant. Many authentic Chinese restaurants will serve sliced lotus root in addition to other vegetables in stir-fry or hot pot dishes. Lotus root can also be steamed and baked. Lotus root has a mild flavor, and crunchy texture almost like a water chestnut. The rhizome is somewhat fibrous and similar to the crisp fibrous texture of celery. Braising, stewing, and other longer cooking methods will help reduce the stringiness.

You can eat lotus leaves when young and tender, but Chinese cooks look forward to using the large sturdy leaves to wrap a filling of sticky rice with chicken and mushrooms. *Lo mai gai*, as this dish is known, is a part of every dim sum menu. The slightly fragrant leaves impart a mild tea-like flavor to the dish. Flower stems are tender and are delicious sliced and cooked. Both seedpods and seeds can be eaten. For a healthful snack, simply pop the seeds out of the pod, peel them, and eat fresh. Like other edible flowers, lotus flower petals are fragrant with a mild sweetness. You can also successfully preserve all parts of the plant by drying.

VEGETARIAN LOTUS ROOT AND VEGETABLE STIR-FRY

My sister, Lisa, shared this vegetarian recipe, which she says is both foolproof and flexible. She typically throws in whatever combination of vegetables she has on hand—such as carrots, wood ear, snap peas, celery, and even edible flowers like daylily buds. She'll also vary the flavor by adding shallots, garlic, or a small handful of chopped cilantro. The addition of sliced lotus root makes this version particularly nutritious, delicious, and attractive. The mushroom seasoning provides a rich umami flavor. It is usually available at Asian supermarkets and some health food stores, but if you can't find it, season lightly with salt instead.

SERVES 4

2 tablespoons corn or peanut oil

2 medium carrots, thinly sliced on the diagonal

2 shallots, thinly sliced

1½ cups lotus root, peeled and sliced ⅛ inch thin

1½ cups snow peas

½ cup dried wood ear, soaked in warm water for 1 hour and then roughly sliced

½ tablespoon mushroom seasoning

1 tablespoon sweet soy sauce

1. Heat the oil in a wok over medium-high heat. When hot, add the carrots and shallots and stir quickly. Cover and cook for about 2 minutes so carrots can begin to soften.

2. Add the lotus root, snow peas, wood ear, and mushroom seasoning. Continue to stir-fry until all vegetables are crisp-tender, about 8 minutes. When the vegetables are cooked, add the sweet soy sauce, toss in the wok, and serve with steamed white rice.

Luffa acutangula (angled luffa gourd)
Luffa cylindrica (smooth luffa gourd)

luffa gourd

絲
瓜

MANDARIN *sīguā*
CANTONESE *si gwaa*

Natural sponges typically come in two forms—the dark buff-colored rounds that come from the sea and the elongated fibrous bath scrubbers that come from the earth. It's hard to believe that the luffa gourds I grow to use in crafts and to dry as natural sponges are the same nutritious vegetables that my parents cook for dinner. Luffa, high in fiber and vitamin C, is well-known in Chinese medicine as an anti-inflammatory and excellent blood purifier. It is also believed to relieve dryness within the body.

Luffa gourds can be angled or smooth, and both types are edible. Angled luffa, the type more commonly used for eating, looks almost like extremely long okra (and is sometimes referred to as Chinese okra) with its ridges and skinny elongated shape. A typical angled luffa is about 18 inches in length and 2 inches in diameter.

Smooth luffa, sometimes called sponge or dishcloth luffa, does not have ridges and makes a better sponge because of its larger circumference. Smooth luffas at maturity are about 12 inches long and 3 inches wide. The absence of ridges on this smooth variety also makes it easier to eventually peel and unveil the sponge, which is the skeleton of the fruit. When immature these fruits are a delicious vegetable; 'Edible Ace' is a popular variety with my Taiwanese friends.

IN THE GARDEN Luffa is an extremely prolific vining plant that can grow up to 15 feet. Plan to provide a sunny spot in the garden, warm soil to sow your seed, a long growing season, and a trellis for it to climb. By summer, sunny yellow flowers will dot the well-established vine. Fruits quickly follow.

Where seasons are short, get a head start by starting luffa seedlings indoors, planting out when the soil warms to at least 70 degrees Fahrenheit. Provide plenty of water to keep the luffa vine healthy. Luffa gourds grow fairly quickly, so begin checking for harvests regularly when the fruits reach 4–6 inches. If allowed to

luffa sponges

To grow luffa as sponges, simply allow them to mature on the vine until the end of the growing season or until they have completely dried out, whichever comes first. When they're completely dry, the outer skin will be brown and you will hear the seeds rattling around inside if you shake the lightweight luffa. If your season is not long enough, simply harvest them before your first freeze and let them dry for a few weeks in a warm dry spot indoors. Peel the outer skin and rinse under running water. Squeeze any remaining pulp through the sponge, shake the seeds out, and then allow to fully dry.

Smooth luffas are the type typically grown for bath sponges.

grow to their full length, luffa gourds can reach 12–24 inches, but they should be harvested for eating at the immature stage. Luffa gourds can get bitter and increasingly tough as they mature.

IN THE KITCHEN Harvest and eat luffa gourds young when they are most tender and mild in taste. To prepare angled luffa for cooking, pare off the hard ridges with a vegetable peeler. The thin green skin that remains after removing the ridges leaves a pretty striped pattern on the vegetable. Then cut the luffa into coins, dice it, or chop it into large bite-sized pieces. Luffa is ideal for any method of cooking from stir-frying to braising, but because the gourd is so tender, it

Angled luffa is a good choice for eating. Pare off the ridges along the length of the luffa before cooking.

is best not to overcook. This versatile mid-summer vegetable works well with chicken, pork, or seafood; try it in any dish that calls for zucchini. One of my mom's summertime dishes is a colorful combination of the easy-to-love luffa gourd with marinated shrimp and the frilly wood ear mushroom.

LUFFA GOURD AND SHRIMP STIR-FRY

Marinating the shrimp in this recipe adds flavor as well as prevents the shrimp from sticking together when cooking. Wood ear is a unique, traditional and medicinal ingredient found in many Chinese dishes. I love the vibrant splash of black of the ruffled wood ear next to the pale green luffa pieces. Like many stir-fries, more time will be spent in preparing this dish than cooking it because luffa gourd is a very tender vegetable that requires just a few minutes of cooking time. Angled luffa is the best choice for cooking, but you could also use a young smooth luffa—or substitute bottle gourd or fuzzy melon.

SERVES 4 AS A SIDE DISH

2   teaspoons cornstarch

1   teaspoon Shaoxing rice wine

1   teaspoon dark (toasted) sesame oil

   Pinch of salt

⅓   pound shrimp, peeled and deveined

2–3 tablespoons corn or peanut oil

1   teaspoon minced ginger

1   teaspoon minced garlic

2   small luffa gourds, peeled and cut into chunks

6   pieces dried wood ear, soaked in water until soft, about 1 hour

1. Stir 1 teaspoon of the cornstarch into ¼ cup of water. Set aside.

2. Combine the rice wine, the remaining 1 teaspoon cornstarch, sesame oil, and a pinch of salt in a large bowl. Add the shrimp and marinate for about 20 minutes at room temperature.

3. Heat a wok over medium-high heat and add 2 tablespoons of the oil. When hot, add the shrimp and quickly stir-fry until just cooked, about 2 minutes. Remove and set aside.

4. Add another tablespoon of oil to the wok if necessary. When hot, add the ginger, garlic, luffa gourd, wood ear, and a pinch of salt. Stir and cover for about a minute until the luffa gourd softens a bit. Add the shrimp and cornstarch solution. When sauce thickens and bubbles, remove from the heat. Serve with steamed white rice.

Basella alba

malabar spinach

MANDARIN *cáncài*
CANTONESE *saan choy*

潺菜

My friend Grace, for whom Asian vegetables are exotic, was surprised to find out that Malabar spinach is an Asian green. Though it's been grown in China for many generations, it is also used in India where it is known as bayam. Other cultures may know this type of spinach as basella or Ceylon spinach.

The reasons to grow Malabar spinach are plentiful. This pretty vining plant does equally well rambling across a garden bed or climbing up a trellis. It grows into a spreading mound in my father's large open garden, but also sits in a container on Grace's patio with its vines trellised, and glossy leaves fresh for cutting year round. The dark green fleshy leaves are strong and generally pest-free. Malabar spinach has either red or green stems and is sometimes sold simply as "red-stemmed" or "green-stemmed." The red-stemmed variety grows more prolifically and is certainly more ornamental. When other varieties of spinach have bolted, Malabar spinach is still thriving trouble-free throughout the long summer. Malabar spinach is rich in vitamins A and C, iron, calcium, and fiber.

IN THE GARDEN An ideal summer vegetable, Malabar spinach thrives in the heat and sun. Because it can take 2–3 weeks for seeds to germinate, it may be a good idea to start seeds indoors with some heat and transplant into the garden when the soil has thoroughly warmed. This allows for a longer growing and harvesting season. Give these climbing plants a trellis or tie plants to a bean pole. Alternatively, you can allow plants to ramble in rows, but provide about 18 inches between plants for a little more growing room. If any long shoots outgrow their space in the garden, cut them back to keep the plants growing neatly.

After about 4 weeks you can begin harvesting. Simply cut leaves off the plants, leaving at least one-third of the plant intact. Once the plants reach the height of their support, prune back the tops of the plants to encourage side shoots to form. Later in the season, bluish flowers

Malabar spinach is an easy-to-grow vining plant that thrives throughout summer when it's too hot and days are too long for other varieties of spinach.

produce shiny red berries that mature to a purplish black. Though pretty, this plant will re-seed itself in ideal climates; to prevent unwanted plants remove and save the seeds, or cut off the seedheads. Chinese artisans have traditionally used the small red berries that the plants produce as food coloring and dyes for crafts.

IN THE KITCHEN You can eat Malabar spinach raw in salads, though most Chinese people cook their greens. The first time my daughter tried a leaf raw, she reported that it was foaming in her mouth. Not a pleasant description, and definitely an exaggeration, this sensation is because of the green's mucilaginous quality, which may equate to a slipperiness when cooked. As such, Malabar spinach can be a great thickening agent for soups. Try adding some slivered Malabar spinach to the bottom of a bowl before ladling hot soup over top. The heat is enough to wilt the spinach, creating a healthful light meal.

In my family, we tend to eat Malabar spinach as we eat many greens—blanched, then topped with oyster sauce and garnished with fried garlic. Malabar spinach is also delicious sautéed, stir-fried, or added to any recipe that calls for a mild leafy green like spinach.

Vigna radiata

mung beans

MANDARIN *lǜdòu*
CANTONESE *luk dao*

綠
豆

The green mung bean is a nutritional powerhouse. Because of this, they are often a first food for babies, and are also an easily digestible bean for ailing adults. Their versatility contributes to their well-deserved popularity. When fresh, they are eaten like snow peas or as shelled peas; dried, they can be cooked like any other legume or processed into mung bean flour, which in turn can be processed into noodles.

IN THE GARDEN Mung beans are easy-to-grow annuals and are unbothered by most pests. In the late spring, after the last frost and when the soil warms to about 60 degrees Fahrenheit, directly sow seeds about 1 inch deep and 4–6 inches apart in a sunny spot in the garden. The plants do vine a bit and would grow well against a fence or supportive structure. Mung bean plants can grow to about five feet tall.

Pods will appear within about 60 days. If harvesting to eat like fresh green beans, pick when the beans are just beginning to show inside the pod. If harvesting to eat like fresh peas, pick when the beans are plump inside the pod, but still green. For dried beans, allow about 90 days. At that point, the plant will be dry and

brown—if you shake the pods, you will hear the dried mung beans rattling around inside. Shell the beans and be sure they are completely dry before storing in an airtight container in a cool, dry place.

IN THE KITCHEN Because mung beans are not really sweet in taste, but are still pleasantly mild and slightly nutty, they are extremely versatile in the kitchen. They can be made into a sweet bean paste and used as an alternative to red bean paste in a variety of sweet treats. Additionally, you can cook mung beans in a healthy porridge, or use them in recipes instead of lentils or other legumes.

Mung beans can also be processed into many other foods, including a favorite, bean thread noodles. Also

Mung beans are made into many different foods, from sweet pastry fillings to flour and noodles.

called cellophane noodles, they are delicious cooked with vegetables or in noodle soup dishes. One of my junk food addictions is an instant noodle soup bowl product called crystal noodles. The name probably refers to the clear mung bean noodle. The spicy tofu variety is my flavor of choice.

The bean sprouts sold in supermarkets are usually sprouted mung beans. Mung bean sprouts are a nutritious addition to many dishes: eat them raw, toss them in salads, or add them to stir-fries.

Vigna angularis

red beans

紅豆

MANDARIN *hóngdòu*
CANTONESE *hung dao*

Also called adzuki beans, red beans are widely used in Chinese sweets. The ¼-inch oblong, shiny red beans have a mild nutty taste and are also somewhat sweet. These beans are nutritious and contain as much as 25 percent protein along with other vitamins and minerals. Red beans have many uses in the kitchen and are eaten in different stages of growth. With their purple-yellow flowers, this bushy plant is just as attractive as it is healthful.

IN THE GARDEN Red bean plants are easy-to-grow annuals with few pests. They are not too fussy about soil requirements and only ask for full sun. In the late spring, after the last frost and when the soil begins to warm, directly sow seeds about 1 inch deep and 4–6 inches apart. The plants do vine a bit and would grow well against a fence or supportive structure. They will grow about 2 feet tall.

Pods will appear within about 60 days. If harvesting to eat like fresh green beans, pick when the beans are just beginning to show inside the pod. If harvesting to eat like fresh peas, pick when beans are plump inside the pod, but still green. For dried beans, allow about 90 days. At that point, the plant will be dry and brown, and the beans will rattle around inside their pods. Shell the beans and be sure they are completely dry before storing in an airtight container in a cool, dry place.

IN THE KITCHEN Red beans aren't very hard so they don't require soaking or cooking for long periods of time before using. They are almost always used in desserts rather than savory dishes. Chinese desserts are typically not as sweet as the desserts of other cultures and the red bean is an ingredient of choice in many treats. Chinese bakeries will usually offer different kinds of breads and pastries made with red bean paste—a smooth concoction made from boiled, mashed, and sweetened red beans.

A delicious and light summer treat is red bean ice (*hung dao bing*

Sweetened red bean paste is a favorite filling for pastries and baked goods.

in Cantonese or *hóng dòu bīng* in Mandarin). One of my favorite Hong Kong–style cafes makes this drink-dessert hybrid by starting with about ¼ pound of boiled, slightly crushed and sweetened red beans in a tall cup. This is topped with a blend of shaved ice and evaporated milk, and served with a wide straw. My parents like to make a slightly sweet soup with red beans and other medicinal ingredients. It's extremely soothing on a cold winter's day or after a formal Chinese banquet dinner.

HOMEMADE RED BEAN PASTE

Red bean paste is a quintessential ingredient in many Chinese desserts, such as filled mochi, ice cream bars, moon cakes, and any number of baked treats. I like to use it as a filling for fried sesame seed balls like the ones from my favorite dim sum restaurant.

MAKES ABOUT 1½ CUPS

1 cup dried red beans

⅓ cup sugar

2 tablespoons canola or corn oil

1. Soften dried red beans by covering with water and soaking overnight, or by boiling beans in water, and then removing from heat, covering, and allowing to sit for 1 hour.

2. After beans have soaked, drain soaking liquid. Add beans to a medium saucepan, cover with about 6 cups water, and bring to a boil. Reduce heat to medium-low and simmer for about 1½ hours until beans have softened and can be easily mashed. Drain.

3. Process beans in a food processor until smooth. Add sugar and process until combined.

4. Add the oil to a wok or frying pan over medium-low heat. Add pureed beans to wok and fry, stirring and pressing with the back of a spatula until beans dry out, forming a thick paste. Allow to cool before using. It will keep in the refrigerator for a week.

Glycine max

soybeans

MANDARIN *huángdòu*
CANTONESE *wong dao*

黄
豆

Fans of soybeans can rely on seeing the protein-packed snack known as eda-mame on the menu of most Japanese restaurants. This Japanese name literally means stem bean, referring to the practice of steaming the soybean pods on the stem. Since people have learned about the health benefits and delicious nutty taste of edamame, its popularity has exploded and you can find it frozen or ready to eat in most supermarkets. My family loves to snack on a big bowl of freshly steamed and salted edamame. To eat, just squeeze one of the fat pods filled with tender beans into your mouth and discard the pod. It's a healthful garden-to-table snack that is even better when enjoyed communally.

IN THE GARDEN Soybeans are incredibly easy to grow, and I have never had an issue with pests or diseases. Gardeners will appreciate that it is a nitrogen-fixing plant as well. When the soil has warmed to about 70 degrees Fahrenheit, sow seeds about 1½ inches deep and 6 inches apart,

Steamed and salted soybeans is an increasingly popular healthy snack.

directly in the garden. Rows should be approximately 24 inches apart. In zones with a shorter warm season, you can start seeds indoors and transplant after soil warms to at least 65 degrees Fahrenheit. To save a step, you can also try direct sowing early soybeans such as 'Midori Giant' (70 days) or the great-tasting 'Envy' (75 days). If your plants grow very tall or heavy with many pods, just loosely tie each plant to a stake so they don't fall over. I like to grow a lot of soybeans and planting them successively ensures we have gradual harvests over the course of several weeks.

To harvest the soybeans for green shelling, pick when the beans bulge in their pods. If desired, till spent plants into the garden soil. This will provide nitrogen to your garden for the next crop. To harvest soybeans as dried beans, wait until the plants turn completely brown. At this point, pull them up and allow them to dry completely in a shed or other dry covered area.

IN THE KITCHEN Fresh whole soybeans are easy to cook: just steam or boil for about 15 minutes or so until the beans inside are tender. Sprinkle with sea salt to serve. To eat, hold the pod near your mouth and squeeze to pop out the beans. Soybeans are great this way, and are often enjoyed with a beer or small cup of sake. Alternatively, fresh soybeans can be blanched and then shelled for use in other dishes such as salads, rice dishes, or stir-fry combinations. You can substitute soybeans in any recipe that calls for lima beans or fava beans.

With more involved preparation, mature, dried soybeans can be made into an incredible number of foods such as tofu cakes, bean curd, tofu sheets, soy milk, tempeh, sprouts, soy sauce, miso, and much more. One of my favorite desserts is a bowl of extremely velvety soft tofu topped with a ladleful of thin, sweet, and gingery syrup. I don't consider my dim sum lunch complete until a server has pushed a cart with this warm treat on it in my direction.

EDAMAME FRIED RICE

Freshly cooked rice is too wet and sticky to make a good fried rice. It also absorbs too much oil. Cold leftover rice will give you the texture you want. Also, resist the urge to stir and move the rice around too much when cooking. Letting the rice keep contact with the wok gives it the flavor and *wok hay* (the breath of the wok) that only restaurant kitchens with high flames can produce. If you like, add some chopped Chinese barbequed roast pork or a couple of chopped Chinese sausages.

SERVES 4–6

4 cups cold cooked rice

3–4 tablespoons corn or peanut oil

4 eggs, lightly beaten

½-inch piece of ginger, peeled and minced

2 cloves garlic, minced

1 cup steamed, shelled edamame

6 scallions, thinly sliced

2 teaspoons dark (toasted) sesame oil

3 tablespoons soy sauce

Salt and black pepper

1. Put cooked leftover rice in a big bowl and break up any clumps of rice so grains are fairly separate.

2. Heat 1 tablespoon of the oil in a wok or large pan over medium-high heat. When hot, add the eggs and stir to scramble; remove the eggs from the wok when still slightly runny. Add 2 or 3 more tablespoons of oil to the wok along with the ginger and garlic. Cook for about 30 seconds, until fragrant, and then add the rice. Give a quick stir and then spread rice up the sides of the wok to fry evenly. Allow to cook undisturbed for 2–3 minutes.

3. Add the cooked eggs, edamame, and scallions, and stir to combine. When hot, drizzle the sesame oil and soy sauce over the rice and stir until incorporated. Add salt and pepper to taste and serve.

Ipomoea batatas

sweet potato greens

MANDARIN *hóngshǔ cài*
CANTONESE *hung she choy*

紅薯菜

As I leave my parents' house every weekend, they often load up my car with edible goodies to take home. Usually it's a dozen chicken or duck eggs, sometimes a bag of Asian pears. On one autumn evening many years ago, my father handed me a large box filled with about 50 pounds of white sweet potatoes. I thought he was being very generous with this particularly large quantity of food and I attempted to convince him to save them for himself. This is when he explained that the real treat was the sweet potato greens he'd been harvesting all summer. The tubers were simply a by-product of the harvest. Now that I know the secret, sweet potato greens are among my favorite Asian greens to eat too. They're mild, tender, and extremely easy to grow, especially when most other greens have bolted in the summer.

Being high in vitamins C and K, folates, and iron, the leaves of the sweet potato plant are actually more nutritious than the tubers themselves, and are usually pest-free all summer. At the end of a long season of harvesting the leaves, the sweet potatoes are a bonus.

We harvest the perfect leafy greens of sweet potato plants all summer long.

sweet potato tubers

Although the greens will grow well in most soils, I'm a fan of sweet potatoes so I also keep the tubers in mind when I'm planning my garden. I always have success with good crops of sweet potatoes when I plant them in loose soil either in hills or along a ridge about 12 inches high. By early fall, when the weather begins to cool, the tubers will be ready for harvest. Dig carefully with a garden fork and allow them to dry out in the sun for a few hours. Cure them in a warm place at about 80 degrees Fahrenheit for 10 days, and then store in a cool, dry place until ready to eat.

IN THE GARDEN My family grows a white heirloom sweet potato that has been passed on from friend to friend. Although the flesh is not as sweet and buttery as a traditional red or orange sweet potato, the leaves are tastier. While all sweet potato leaves are edible, some varieties taste better than others. I have seen vendors sell sweet potato slips (rooted cuttings) as "Asian greens variety." Aside from asking a sweet potato vendor to recommend a variety that produces tasty greens, the best way to see which you like best may be to test different varieties on your own. After that, it is easy to save a few seed potatoes to grow the following year. Another way to find a good variety is to try starting your own plants by buying sweet potato leaves from a farmer's market or Asian supermarket. Leaves will often root easily after sitting in a glass of water for a week or two and can then be transplanted into the garden.

The most common way to grow sweet potato plants is to purchase slips directly from a sweet potato farmer or vendor. Even when slips look worse for the wear after being shipped, they bounce back quickly once planted. Another method is to start your own slips with some healthy, unblemished sweet potato tubers about 3 months before your last frost date. Place the potato into a jar of water so that about half sits in the water and half sits above the water. Aim for a few eyes (the divots that sprouts grow from) to sit above the water. Use bamboo barbeque skewers or toothpicks stuck into the side of the potato to help keep the sweet potato in place. Once you see leaves from some healthy shoots

While it is rewarding to dig for sweet potatoes in the fall, you can harvest the nutritious leaves of the plant all summer.

My whole family loves the texture and taste of my mom's cooked sweet potato greens, especially when seasoned simply with a couple splashes of oyster sauce.

growing from the top of the sweet potato, remove the shoots carefully from the potato and place them in a cup of water. In a few days, they will root. Keep the water in the cup fresh, changing whenever the water begins to look murky. When the roots are about 1 inch long, plant the slips in the garden about 12 inches apart in small hills. (Alternatively, purchase sweet potato slips.) Plant slips about 4 weeks after the date of last frost, when soil has warmed to at least 60 degrees Fahrenheit.

In the first few weeks, water well but gently so that the hills don't erode. A thick layer of mulch will also help keep the soil in place. Within a month, each plant will grow into a neat lush mound. Begin harvesting once each plant has numerous leaves and has filled out, leaving about one-third of the plant intact.

IN THE KITCHEN Sweet potato greens are typically boiled, sautéed, or stir-fried. My mom once made a dish that appeared to be a very slim type of green bean I'd never seen before. No one could guess the vegetable. Turns out, she had cut just the stems from the sweet potato greens, and stir-fried them for an interesting vegetable dish. For a more traditional family favorite, greens are washed, boiled in a large pot of water for several minutes until tender, drained, and then topped with oyster sauce, soy sauce, or another favorite sauce. Adding a sautéed aromatic, such as garlic, shallots, or onions, boosts the flavor of this delicious, mild, and nutritious vegetable.

FALL

秋
天

In the fall, when leaves turn yellow and orange against dark trunks and branches, when my summer-blooming flowers are done, when my vegetable garden is eking out some last peppers and tomatoes while the rest of it begins to brown and dry up, my father's garden is green, lush, and still fantastic. It's as if the cooler weather and shorter days had no effect on his garden. Heads of cabbage are picture perfect. Leafy greens are ready to be plucked for salads. Winter squash are heavy and prime for fall soups. How can this be?

Far too often, I realize that I missed the narrow window of opportunity during the late summer when I should have been ►

Abundant yellow bottle gourd flowers cover the vine while maturing double-bulbed gourds hang from a sturdy trellis. After this stage, the gourds will begin to dry out and can be used for decorative or household purposes.

tending to those longer-season vegetables, planning for my fall garden, cleaning up spent plants, and sowing seeds for a fall harvest that could arguably be the best crop of the year. Fall gardens don't just magically happen.

fall planting

To figure out the timing of this window of opportunity, think about when you want to harvest your crop. For any tender vegetables that may be easily killed by frost, the harvest period should be before the date of first frost for your zone. To calculate your seed-starting date, look at the number of days to maturity on your seed packet. Add 7 days to account for seed germination. Since days are cooler and shorter in the fall, add another 14 days to make up for the short-day factor. Finally, take this total and count backward from the date that you expect to be harvesting that vegetable. This is the approximate date to start sowing seeds directly in the garden for a fall crop of vegetables. Root vegetables are best when sown directly in the garden so they're not disturbed as they grow.

If you plan to start seeds indoors to transplant as seedlings, add another 4–6 weeks because the days-to-maturity guideline begins either from the time seeds germinate directly in the garden, or when transplants are set out. It will take these extra weeks to raise seedlings to a healthy size for transplanting. You can start most lettuces and cabbages indoors and transplant them in the early fall. Sometimes, hot summer days prevent seeds of these plants from germinating, or even once germinated, weather factors mean temperamental Asian lettuces send up their tall stalks and bolt before they ever get to enjoy those cool fall days. You can prevent this problem by starting fall vegetables inside and transplanting once they're established and the heat of summer wanes.

Asian leafy greens are particularly excellent in the fall as compared to late spring when aphids may attack or summer when fungal diseases may be rampant and Asian greens are prone to bolting. The combination of less-stressful gardening conditions, cooler weather, and shorter days creates the environment for lush, leafy greens that look perfect for months. Some greens, such as tatsoi, taste even sweeter in the fall after leaves have been hit with a frost.

succession planting

While other gardens may become sparse throughout the season or sputter out by late summer, you can have a steady harvest of vegetables by practicing succession planting. Quick growing, cool-weather vegetables such as radishes,

If you sow pea seeds frequently enough, you will have a continuous supply to harvest.

Rows of stem lettuce sown in succession provide a long season of harvest.

stem lettuce, snow pea sprouts, and all the leafy greens in this chapter do well with this technique. To plant successively, sow seeds frequently enough to have a continuous and uninterrupted supply of vegetables to harvest. This may mean sowing a row of bok choy every 10 days by the calendar, or simply when the previous row has germinated. By the time you are ready to harvest the first crop of bok choy, a second crop will be nearing maturity.

You can sow different crops one after the other to provide a continuous harvest. For example, as soon as your soybean plants mature and you pull them from the garden in late summer, sow your fall greens. Intercropping is another method that maximizes harvests. In the fall garden, this might mean taking advantage of the space in between radishes that might otherwise sit unused by planting a quick-growing, shallow-rooted lettuce such as a choy. With good planning, correct timing, and a variety of succession-planting methods, gardeners can maximize garden space and create a nonstop harvest.

seed saving

The fall season is full of garden activities, including seed saving. As I make my way down my parents' long driveway, I'm always careful not to drive over my father's shallow woven tray containing seeds drying out. Fall is a time for ensuring there will be food next year by saving the seeds of the biggest and best vegetables of this season. Photos abound of my sister and me as kids in late summer or early fall, posing with a super large squash. Every year, my father makes us search for my sister's old basketball to place next to the winter melon so photos will show the enormity of the vegetable. More than likely these gigantic vegetables will be used for seed stock.

When choosing seed stock, it's important to choose from the best plants. Do not use any plants that are diseased or have bolted prematurely. When you have identified the ideal plant, stop watering when the seedpods begin to turn yellow. For plants with seeds that dry up inside their seedpods or flower heads (such as lettuce, beans, and radishes) seed saving is simple. Allow the seedpod or flower head to dry naturally on the plant if possible, or pull them up and hang them to dry indoors if heavy rains, strong wind, or animal pests threaten to ruin plants. When the seedpods are completely dry, crack open the pod, or just shake the seeds onto a screen or tray to dry. Place completely dried seeds in jars or paper envelopes and be sure to label with the seed type and date. Store in a cool, dry, dark place.

Some plants, such as cucumbers, melons, squash, and peppers, contain seeds that are embedded in the damp flesh of the fruits. These seeds may benefit from wet processing, a method that involves a fermentation of the juice, seeds, and flesh. During this process, some of the seed-borne diseases and molds that may be present on the surface of the seeds are wiped out. The fermentation and drying process also removes germination-inhibiting substances on the seed coats of some types of seeds such as tomatoes.

To begin wet processing seeds, scoop out the seeds from the fruits and place in a jar. Pieces of pulp and juice may be included and will be rinsed away later. If the combination of pulp, juice, and seeds is too thick to stir, add a little water so that the mixture is about 25 percent water. Stir and cover the jar with a towel or a piece of plastic wrap with a hole poked in the top. Keep the jar in a warm location and stir once or twice a day. After 4 or 5 days, the mixture will begin to ferment and you may see bubbling and white mold on the surface of the mixture. You may also notice that any gelatinous goop surrounding the seeds has begun to break down. After the fermentation has been occurring for a day or so, it will be time to separate the seeds from the rest of the mixture. Add water to the jar and stir. After a few moments, viable seeds will sink to the bottom and

Seeds saved from a large planting of tatsoi will be viable for the next two years or so.

Store seeds in airtight containers and in a cool, dry, dark place.

poor-quality seeds will float to the top. Slowly pour off the water and floating seeds. Repeat this process by adding more water, stirring, settling, and pouring off, until the water runs clear. Pour seeds through a strainer and then pour them onto a screen in a single layer to air dry. Allow them to dry undisturbed for up to a few weeks before packing them away in airtight jars and storing in a cool, dry, dark place.

Keep in mind that some plants such as bok choy, mizuna, and turnips of the *Brassica rapa* Chinensis Group will cross-pollinate. Different varieties of the same vegetable may also cross-pollinate. Seeds from cross-pollinated plants are not predictable, and usually produce inferior vegetables. If you want to be able to save genetically pure seed, space plants far enough apart so they won't cross-pollinate by wind or insects. The safe distance to sow plants of the same genus varies. For example, lettuce may need only 25 feet whereas eggplants may require 50 feet. For some crops, like peppers, isolation to prevent cross-pollination may be so far that it will not be reasonable for the home gardener to accomplish. Backyard gardeners, especially in neighborhoods with other backyard gardeners, may find it most appropriate to buy new genetically pure seed instead.

The bamboo harvest period is short and intense. Preserving shoots by drying means homegrown bamboo shoots can be rehydrated and used year round.

food preservation

While food preservation was once a necessity for villagers like my parents to survive the cold months in Shandong, it now symbolizes the joy and fortune of having an excess of crops, creating new foods from ordinary vegetables from the garden, and having healthy foods to last until next spring. At their house every fall, my parents preserve duck eggs in salty brine, which will offer a savory zing to one of my go-to comfort foods—pork bone congee. Fish from the pond such as perch or small bass have been sundried and will be preserved in salted oil. My children and I love to eat small pieces of the salty fish in my father's homemade plain, white, steamed buns. My parents laugh as we relish this country food like it is the most delicious fancy dinner my mom has ever cooked.

Aside from her more artisanal food projects, my mom takes on the summer–fall excess as her job. Every summer, it's common to hear her muttering under her breath about how busy she is, washing, blanching, drying, preserving, cooking, freezing, and dehydrating. I always need to talk my mom down as she curses my father for once again, growing too much. When enough has been shared with friends, and enough is set aside for meals, a rich summer needs to be preserved so that no food is wasted.

In the early fall, my parents fill their many food dehydrators with vegetables like sliced radishes, chunks of bottle gourd, or whole peppers. Removing the moisture through the drying process means the vegetables will keep for many months when stored in airtight jars. This assortment of dehydrated vegetables and herbs can be rehydrated and added to stir-fries and other dishes throughout the winter.

My family eats most of the green leafy vegetables we grow (sharing a good crop with the ducks), but it's possible to preserve most other vegetables by drying in some way, including some that might not be expected. One of my favorite idyllic scenes from Asian gardens is a long string of bok choy hanging to air dry like clothes pinned to a clothesline. These dried bundles of bok choy can be added to a bowl of noodles just before hot soup is ladled over it. My zone has high levels of humidity so I prefer to use food dehydrators because fleshy vegetables such as the base of bok choy or a slice of squash can often end up moldy before they dry completely.

Winter melons and some other vegetables will sit for months in a cold cellar or shed, ready to be hacked into large wedges when the weather turns and you have a craving for a nourishing hot pot of soup. Sweet potatoes—producers of those delicious greens we've been enjoying all summer—will be unearthed from the garden sometime before frost, cured for a week or so, and then stored for use throughout the fall.

The fall garden requires some cleanup, but cool weather makes the work pleasant enough.

Fall is also a good time to turn our attention to classic family recipes for pickles and other condiments. We cook chile peppers into a spicy XO sauce (see page 99), which I love using as a condiment with dumplings, to enliven a stir-fry, or atop a plate of my father's homemade noodles. I also look forward to making jars of pickled or fermented goodies with vegetables such as Napa cabbage or radishes.

While it was not a reality during the time my parents grew up, freezing vegetables is another way my parents preserve their harvests today. This method works well with the last pickings of a fall crop of beans, pumpkins, and radishes. Before freezing, rinse vegetables, cut into desired lengths, and then quickly blanch to keep them vibrant-looking, fresh-tasting, and full of nutrition. After blanching, pat the vegetables dry thoroughly, wrap or seal them well, and store in the freezer. These frozen portions of vegetables will provide a much-appreciated taste of summer to fall and winter meals.

garden cleanup

Though cleaning up the garden is not exactly my idea of fun, the crisp autumn air and falling leaves make it a wonderful time of year to be outside. I relish the satisfactory crackle of dried plants when I remove them from the garden. If spent plants are healthy, you can compost them, but any insect-infested or diseased plants should be taken out and discarded with garden waste.

Fallen maple leaves are abundant in my yard. I usually shred and then bag or pile up excess leaves; they will decompose by next spring into a leaf mold that I use to condition the soil in my garden. Another option is to use the shredded leaves as mulch in the vegetable garden. I also like to keep a pile of these brown leaves next to my compost bin year round to mix in with greens like kitchen scraps.

Just one afternoon doing garden cleanup can quickly and visibly neaten the fall garden. This is rewarding in itself, but knowing that a clean garden now means fewer pests and diseases next spring makes the work even more appealing. What's left is a veritable blank canvas outside that remains until next season. That means when I'm cozy and warm inside my house, I can simply look out the window and easily dream up next year's plan.

Lactuca sativa

a choy

MANDARIN *a cài*
CANTONESE *a choy*

This lettuce, also called *mak choy*, is a Taiwanese favorite. It has long, narrow, pointed leaves and a mild and sweet taste that is great cooked or raw. With a similar crisp midrib, a choy looks like a sword-shaped variation of romaine, butterhead, or other common lettuce. Seed suppliers may sell a choy as pointed leaf or sword leaf lettuce. This easy-to-like lettuce thrives in cool weather—my father loads his fall garden with it—and is also heart-healthy with high amounts of beta-carotene, folates, and fiber.

IN THE GARDEN A choy, like other tender Asian greens, is best grown in the fall, because it is prone to bolting when planted in the spring. In mid to late summer, sow seed directly in the garden bed. Either sprinkle seed and rake surface gently, or seed and then just barely cover with a fine layer of soil. Keep soil moist while seeds are germinating by gently watering, but avoid washing the seeds out of place. As with all lettuces, be sure the bed drains well as excess water may lead to bottom rot on the plant. When seedlings have emerged and have a few leaves, thin to about 4 inches apart. Spacing plants as close as 4 inches apart will allow you to easily cut several young plants for use, or even to cut every other plant

for use while letting remaining plants continue to grow. Alternatively, space 8 inches apart so plants have a little more room to grow and harvest outer leaves as needed. A choy should be ready for harvest when about 10 inches tall, in about 6 weeks. You can use this lettuce at any stage but it tastes best when harvested young. For a continuous crop until frost, sow seed successively.

IN THE KITCHEN A choy is probably the Chinese leafy green that most closely resembles common lettuces. The high water content gives it a refreshing taste and this sweet and delicate lettuce can be eaten in salads just like romaine lettuce. Traditionally, it is usually cooked before eating

A choy is a mild Taiwanese lettuce with a great taste similar to romaine.

A choy was sown in the seed bed to the right in order to get an early start while the planting bed to the left was still full of summer vegetables. Now that the summer vegetables are done, the young lettuce plants are being transplanted to neat rows where they'll have room to grow until frost.

The ducks are crazy for a choy and my father treats them to an armful every time he harvests some for himself.

and is just sturdy enough to hold up well. A choy is a versatile Chinese green that can be a healthy ingredient in any favorite recipe. It has a slight hint of bitterness, but it is generally considered a mild leafy green that is wonderful when cut into manageable pieces, quickly sautéed or boiled, and topped with oil and flash-fried garlic. Keep in mind that this vegetable just needs to be cooked until wilted, which should require only a few minutes. To use in a stir-fry or noodle dish, sauté meat and denser vegetables until nearly cooked before adding a choy during the last few minutes.

Brassica rapa Chinensis Group

bok choy

MANDARIN *xiǎo báicài, qīng jiāng cài*
CANTONESE *bok choy*

小白菜 青江菜 白菜

A member of the mustard family, bok choy is probably the most familiar Chinese vegetable. Although the name translates to white vegetable, the dark green leaves grow loosely atop white stalks that meet at the base like wide spoons. Some varieties of bok choy are green-stemmed. Many noodle house soup dishes are punctuated with the bright green color of the tender bok choy. Some may describe the leaves as peppery, but the cooking process tames any bit of bite. Bok choy has no fat or cholesterol and contains a generous amount of vitamins A and C, fiber, protein, folates, calcium, and iron. Bok choy is good for those new to Asian vegetables given its versatility, palatability, beauty, and healthfulness.

Bok choy is a versatile and popular Chinese vegetable with several varieties, each with slight variations in color, size, and shape.

IN THE GARDEN Another factor in bok choy's popularity might be the ease with which it grows. Bok choy is a cold-weather crop that you can grow in the spring, fall, or both. With a short time to maturity, you'll be enjoying your first crop in 30–50 days.

Bok choy can grow to be very tall when mature, but most people prefer to eat it in the baby stage. 'Ching Chiang' is a dwarf, green-stemmed bok choy sought after for its particularly tender leaves and crisp stems. 'Ching Chiang' and other similar varieties are sometimes described as baby bok choy, but they are actually dwarf varieties and not full-sized standard plants at a young stage.

While gardeners can be successful with a quick crop in the cool of the early spring and fall, bok choy is also notoriously finicky, and sometimes it seems any number of factors cause the plant to send up a flower stalk and bolt. The folk wisdom of many cultures associates the bolting of leafy green vegetables like bok choy with too-hot weather. However, the primary factor that determines when bok choy will bolt is light exposure.

Bok choy is a long-day plant and has a critical day length measured by a number of daylight hours. Once the day length is *longer* than the critical day length, the plant will flower and set seed. In the garden, we can't control the daylight, but growing the vegetable in partial shade, and choosing to grow bok choy in the spring and fall when we have shorter days can help.

For a spring crop, start seeds indoors 4–6 weeks before your last frost date. After last frost, transplant seedlings 6–12 inches apart in rows 18–30 inches apart. Space smaller varieties closer together. To grow in the fall, sow seeds directly in the garden about 8 weeks before your first frost date. Plant seeds ¼–½ inch deep about 1 inch apart in wide rows. Keep the planting area consistently moist until seeds have germinated, in about a week. Thin plants to 6–12 inches apart. You can start harvesting bok choy in the baby stage and up to 12–18 inches tall.

IN THE KITCHEN Bok choy is an excellent, all-purpose, mild-tasting Chinese vegetable that goes well in a wide variety of dishes. Traditionally,

Dwarf or baby bok choy can be cut in half lengthwise or simply cooked whole.

bok choy is used in soups or noodle soups, and is also often stir-fried, braised, and boiled in Chinese hot pot meals. In just about any recipe calling for Asian greens, you can substitute bok choy.

If using larger plants, separate the leaves and cut the white stalk from the top of the leaf. Similar to cooking a vegetable like chard, the more mature, thicker sections of stalk may need a longer cooking time so it's a good idea to start by cooking the stalk first before adding the green tops so the whole vegetable cooks evenly. For baby bok choy, it is not necessary to separate the leaves from the stalks or pull the leaves apart from each other. Simply harvest the entire baby plant, wash it thoroughly, and cook whole. This is how the restaurants serve bok choy in the noodle soups I love so much.

STIR-FRIED BOK CHOY AND BEEF

This recipe of my mom's is a simple everyday dish that she's cooked for decades with countless variations. This version calls for a small amount of beef, but you could also use sliced or ground pork, chicken, shrimp, or chunks of fish. For a vegetarian version, add tofu or shiitake mushrooms and mung bean thread noodles. In place of the bok choy, you could substitute almost any other leafy green vegetable such as mustard greens, choy sum, cabbage, or Malabar spinach.

SERVES 4 AS A SIDE DISH

2 tablespoons soy sauce

½ teaspoon sugar

1 teaspoon dark (toasted) sesame oil

1 teaspoon cornstarch

¼ pound beef, like flank steak, cut into thin 2-inch strips across the grain

1 pound bok choy

2–3 tablespoons corn or peanut oil

3 cloves minced garlic

Salt and freshly ground black pepper

1. Combine the soy sauce, sugar, sesame oil, and cornstarch in a bowl. Add the beef and marinate for 30 minutes at room temperature.

2. Cut the bottom half inch or so off the base of the bok choy so that the outer leaves separate. Keep the inner heart intact. Rinse thoroughly and drain.

3. Place a wok over medium-high heat. When hot, add 2 tablespoons of the oil. Add the beef and marinade and stir-fry until just cooked, about 3 minutes. Transfer the meat to a small bowl and set aside.

4. Add another tablespoon of oil to the wok if necessary. When hot, add the bok choy and cook, stirring, for a minute. Add the garlic to the top of the bok choy. Cover and continue to cook over medium heat for 7–10 minutes, turning occasionally. The bok choy is ready when stems are just tender and have turned a bright, bold green.

5. Add the cooked beef and stir until heated through. Season with salt and pepper to taste, and serve.

Brassica rapa Chinensis Group

choy sum

MANDARIN *càixīn*
CANTONESE *choy sum*

菜心

Translated from Cantonese, choy sum means "heart of the vegetable." It is a delicious, attractive, tall, leafy vegetable with white or green stems. It is similar to and eaten like Chinese broccoli gailan—leaves, shoots, flower stalk, flowers, and all. While gailan has more of a bluish-green leaf color, choy sum is green, with oval-shaped leaves that are neater around the edge. It may also be compared to bok choy, but choy sum usually has thinner stems and smaller flower buds upon harvesting.

Choy sum is generally considered more tender and milder than bok choy. It's no wonder choy sum is a favorite vegetable in Hong Kong and Southern China. While its growing popularity in North America means choy sum can be found at international supermarkets and farmer's markets, choy sum wilts quickly after being harvested; another reason it's always better to grow your own. Any white-stemmed variety would be excellent to try.

Health-conscious gardeners will appreciate that choy sum is a particularly nutritious green. It has plenty of beta-carotene, B vitamins, vitamin C, and fiber. Choy sum also offers calcium in a form that is more readily absorbed than other greens like spinach.

IN THE GARDEN Choy sum is a cool-weather crop and does not like extremes in temperature. It will not tolerate frost and is also likely to prematurely bolt the moment it begins to get hot out. Like other brassicas, pests such as aphids, caterpillars, and slugs can be a problem. Grow this fussy but delicious vegetable in the fall in order to have the best chance for success.

Sow seeds directly in the garden 6–8 weeks before your first expected frost. Sprinkle seeds in and cover with a fine layer of soil. Keep soil moist until seeds have germinated. Thin plants to about 6 inches apart. Choy sum roots are shallow, so plants should be cultivated carefully and watered regularly to help the plant stems stay tender.

yu choy

Choy sum is closely related to, and often confused with yu choy, or edible rape, and the two vegetables can be used interchangeably in recipes. People typically refer to this green-stemmed vegetable as green choy sum. Yu choy is grown for its green leaves and stalks and is also harvested just as the plant begins to flower. It is mild and tender like choy sum. 'Yu Choy Sin' is a common and well-liked variety.

Choy sum should be harvested just as the flower buds begin to appear, 40–60 days after sowing. This is when the leaves and stalks will be most tender and sweet. To harvest, simply cut the whole plant, leaves and all. Alternatively, try cutting just the main stalk. The plant will typically send up side shoots, much like broccoli does. Be sure to stay on top of harvesting because older plants will become stringy and tough. I like to plant choy sum successively so I can harvest the entire plant at once with more ready to be cut soon thereafter.

IN THE KITCHEN Choy sum appears all the time on dim sum carts and restaurant menus. When harvested young, the tender stalks can be cut and eaten raw, but like most Chinese vegetables, they are typically cooked first. Choy sum is usually boiled or blanched and then stir-fried. It can be added to noodle dishes and soups but is most often served on a big plate as a featured vegetable dish.

I like to cut choy sum into 2- to 4-inch sections, separating the stem pieces from the leaves. Because the stems require a slightly longer cooking time, they can be blanched in lightly salted water for a few minutes before adding the leaves for just a minute. The leaves turn bright green once drained and then lightly stir-fried.

Extremely popular in Hong Kong and Southern China, choy sum is eaten leaf, stem, flowers, and all.

Coriandrum sativum

cilantro

香菜

MANDARIN *xiāngcài*
CANTONESE *hoeng choy*

Cilantro has been in cultivation for thousands of years and seeds have been found in ancient Egyptian tombs. Though not a native of China, the plant made its way over from surrounding areas a thousand years ago. Since then, it has been a staple in Chinese cuisine. In the United States, the leafy herb is called cilantro while the brown seeds of the plant, known as coriander, are also an important part of the cuisines of many Asian countries. Coriander is a key ingredient in curries. In other parts of the world, the entire plant is often referred to simply as coriander or Chinese parsley.

Growing up, my mom would sometimes send me outside to cut a small bunch of cilantro. I remember kneeling in the garden with cilantro on one side and flat leaf parsley on the other. It was easy to be confused by the similar appearance, but cilantro is an intensely flavorful herb that is immediately identifiable by smell. I could close my eyes and get lost in the strong and citrusy scent of the herb. Beyond the penetrating flavor and fragrance, cilantro provides vitamins A, C, and K, and several antioxidants such as beta-carotene and lutein.

IN THE GARDEN Cilantro is a cool-weather annual herb. The best crops are grown in the fall because cilantro is influenced by both temperature and lengthening days. In my zone 6 garden, cilantro is difficult to grow during the summer partially because of our hot nights. Plants like cilantro need cooler night temperatures in order to tolerate hot days. From time to time, I have been successful with a spring-into-summer patch of cilantro.

These were small patches planted under raspberry canes or next to other tall plants that cast some shade over a bare spot in the garden.

In mid to late summer, sow seed about ¼ inch deep directly in the garden and thin plants to about 4 inches apart. Plants should be at least 6 inches tall before harvesting. Simply cut stems about an inch from the soil line, making sure not to take more than one-third of the plant at

All parts of the cilantro plant are edible—from the roots added to Thai soups to the seeds ground in Indian curries—and give Asian cuisines their characteristic flavors.

a time so the plant can continue to grow.

Because cilantro does bolt easily if the weather gets hot, it may be a good idea to grow a slow-to-bolt variety such as 'Santo', which is also known for having a particularly strong flavor. Planting cilantro successively, especially if growing from spring through fall, can help maximize your chances of having cilantro on hand when you want it.

When cilantro bolts it sends up tall thin stems topped with wispy flat umbels of white flowers that eventually produce coriander seeds. Many gardeners look forward to this stage as much as the leafy harvesting stage because beneficial insects like predatory and parasitic wasps are attracted to its lacy flowers. Attracting beneficial insects helps create a healthier garden with a bigger harvest, so I try to dedicate about 10 percent of the space in each of my vegetable garden beds to growing plants that attract beneficial insects. Bolted cilantro is welcome to stay in my garden for that purpose.

Gardeners who love coriander seeds may seek out varieties that are bred to bolt quickly for an abundant harvest of seeds. To harvest seeds, wait until the seedheads begin to brown and dry and then cut the stem. Place upside down in a brown paper bag for about a week until fully dry. Seed husks will split open and coriander seeds will fall into the bag.

IN THE KITCHEN Cilantro is a frequently used herb in Indian, Mexican, and Chinese dishes. Its strong fragrance pairs well with all meats, many vegetables, soups, and stews. In Chinese cuisine, it adds a familiar flavor to soups and many cold dishes. Cilantro is occasionally added while cooking, but it is most often added near the end of the cooking time, stirred into the dish just before serving, or chopped and sprinkled as a flavorful garnish. Being a cool-weather crop, cilantro and soups or congees are natural partners. One of my favorite comfort foods is a large bowl of rice congee (fish and ginger, pork, or maybe just some salted duck egg) with a generous topping of chopped cilantro on top. Cilantro also offers some fresh green color when used as a garnish.

cilantro root

Although bunches of cilantro are commonly found in all supermarkets, cilantro root is not: another benefit of growing your own food. Frequently used in Thai cuisine, cilantro root imparts a mild herbal flavor. Before using, wash the root and bottom inch of the stems. You can add the whole chunk to a pot of soup, or chop it up and crush it along with ingredients like galangal, peppers, and garlic to create the base for a homemade curry paste.

All parts of the cilantro plant are edible. In Chinese cooking, both stems and leaves are used, roughly chopped or simply cut into lengths. Western recipes generally call for cilantro leaves to be chopped or cut into shorter lengths, while stems are often not desired.

Coriander seeds taste similar to cilantro but have a much different use. Seeds are popular in Indian cuisine and are an important component in garam masala, in which the seeds are ground first. Coriander is also added to curry and goes well with chicken, beef, and other meats. Roasting the seeds before using intensifies the nutty, spicy, orangey-lime flavor, and is the first step in making an Indian sambhar. Coriander seeds are also high in the phytochemicals that prevent food from spoiling, making it a tasty and useful addition to recipes like pickles.

STEAMED SEA BASS WITH CILANTRO, GINGER, AND SCALLIONS

One of my father's favorite pastimes is fishing, and because his 6-acre pond is just steps from his house, a fish dinner could not be fresher. We have enjoyed this quick dish with many types of fish from his pond or fishing excursions, or from the market. I suggest sea bass for this recipe, but snapper, flounder, or just about any fresh or saltwater fish will work. The combination of cilantro, ginger, scallions, and a little soy sauce gives this dish a light and clean taste that is distinctively Chinese.

SERVES 4

1 (1½-pound) whole sea bass or other fish, scaled and cleaned, with head and tail on

Salt and black pepper

⅓ cup corn or peanut oil

2-inch section of ginger, peeled and julienned

½ cup light soy sauce

1 tablespoon Shaoxing rice wine

Small bunch of cilantro, cut into 2-inch sections

3 scallions or bunching onions, cut into 2-inch pieces and julienned

1. Place fish on a heatproof plate (like a pie plate) that will fit inside a large pot or wok. Season on both sides with salt and pepper.

2. Add a steamer basket or rack to a pot or wok. Fill the pot with water to just below the bottom of the steamer basket. Bring the water to a boil over high heat. Position the plate of fish in the steamer basket. Cover the pot and steam for 10–15 minutes until the thickest part of the fish is done. The fish should be opaque and flaky when poked with the tip of a knife. Remove carefully and set aside.

3. Heat the oil in a small saucepan. Stir-fry the ginger for just a minute until fragrant. Add the soy sauce, rice wine, cilantro, and scallions, and cook for 1–2 more minutes until the scallions and cilantro soften up a bit. Pour the sauce over the fish to serve.

Brassica oleracea

gailan

芥蘭

MANDARIN *jièlán*
CANTONESE *gai laan*

Once you've tasted gailan, which my sister describes as "asparagus's cousin," it's difficult to name a more delicious vegetable. Similar in appearance to broccoli raab (and often called Chinese broccoli), all parts are edible and equally delicious. Everyone in our family has a favorite section. Some like the thick, glossy leaves that turn soft but still substantive when cooked; my older daughter and I prefer the thick stems that are just crisp-tender when cooked perfectly.

The fleshy stems and dark green leaves of cooked gailan is an elegant and often pricey vegetable dish in Chinese restaurants. Rich in vitamins, iron, and calcium, gailan is particularly nutritious when homegrown and harvested just before cooking. 'Ryokuho' is a tall variety with the thick stems we covet. 'Green Lance' and 'South Sea' are early maturing varieties, ready in about 40 days.

All parts of this tender, slightly bitter vegetable—a family favorite—are edible.

Gailan's blue-green leaves look perfect when cooked. An easy and great-tasting method is to boil the greens until tender and then top them with oyster sauce and fried garlic.

IN THE GARDEN Gailan can tolerate a light frost and loves cool weather and consistent moisture. Because it can become susceptible to pests and hot-weather bolting, we typically only grow gailan as a fall crop, planting successively in mid to late summer to keep this vegetable primed for continuous harvesting.

In mid to late summer, sow seeds about ½ inch deep and in rows 12 inches apart. Gailan grows to about 18 inches tall. If you plan to harvest the plant whole when young, thin plants to about 8 inches apart. If you are going to harvest just the main flowering shoot, in which case the plant will produce secondary shoots, consider giving plants a little more room to grow.

Gailan is prized for its blue-green leaves and young flowering stems, and tastes best just prior to the flowers opening. At harvest time, gailan will have a loose, leafy appearance with flowering shoots about ½ inch in diameter. Leaves will have a slightly waxy look. Although the greens don't appear as vibrant in the garden as some other Chinese greens, they will be beautiful when cooked.

IN THE KITCHEN A common and easy way to cook and serve gailan is to boil the long green until tender, pile neatly on a serving plate, and top with a few generous shakes of oyster sauce and flash-fried garlic (along with the oil it was fried in). Gailan is delicious when served in this traditional way. Though a star on its own, gailan is versatile enough to be used in any meat, seafood, or vegetable recipe that calls for broccoli or another Asian green.

GAILAN WITH GARLIC AND OYSTER SAUCE

This is my mom's master recipe for greens. Gailan is my favorite, but this recipe works for pretty much every green leafy vegetable including watercress, Malabar spinach, sweet potato greens, choy sum, and tatsoi. Tender, leafier greens can take just 30 seconds to cook whereas greens with thick stems like gailan need up to a few minutes. The best way to know when they're tender is to taste them. Or, you can rely on my mom's trick: if she can easily stab her thumbnail into the thick stem, it's done. For vegetarians, vegetarian oyster sauce, usually made from mushrooms, is available at Asian supermarkets.

SERVES 4

1 pound gailan or other greens, rinsed and dried

¼ cup oyster sauce

3 tablespoons corn or peanut oil

5 cloves garlic, chopped

1. Bring a large pot of water to boil over high heat. Add the greens and cook until tender, 30 seconds to a few minutes, depending on type. Remove the greens with a Chinese skimmer (or tongs or a slotted spoon) and place on a serving plate. They may be a little wet and that's okay. Top with the oyster sauce.

2. Heat the oil until hot in a frying pan. Add the garlic and fry until golden and fragrant, 1–2 minutes. Pour the oil and garlic onto the greens. Serve family style with rice and other dishes.

Zingiber officinale

ginger

羌

MANDARIN *jiāng*
CANTONESE *geung*

Ginger is an incredibly versatile root used to spice up savory stir-fries, desserts, drinks, and more. A piece of ginger candy or a ginger-spiced drink is a common home remedy to settle a queasy stomach. Ginger is also known for being warming to the body. Beyond all the comforting qualities of ginger, I just love the sharp flavor of the root. My favorite ways to enjoy it are julienned in my parents' fresh fish congee or crushed with scallions and served as a dipping sauce with a fragrant anise chicken. I also love desserts like the sweetened ginger-steeped broth that is the base for mochi balls filled with sesame paste. When it's cold out, I also like to sip on a sweet and robust orange peel and ginger drink served at my local Hong Kong–style cafe.

IN THE GARDEN The ginger plant thrives in climates with a long hot summer. A moist but not soggy spot in the garden under filtered sunlight or shade in tropical or subtropical zones 9–12 is ideal. In Southern China,

A flavorful and healthful root, ginger spices up many dishes.

Ginger's zing is delicious in savory dishes, sweet baked treats and desserts, or simply sliced and candied on its own.

ginger is an understory plant as too much sun may prevent rhizomes from growing.

Purchase rhizomes at farmer's markets or from seed suppliers. Be sure rhizomes are fresh and are not dried out, or have not been previously frozen as supermarket ginger may have been. In early spring, prepare fresh rhizomes for planting by cutting into smaller 2-inch sections, making sure each piece has a few growing eyes. Allow cuts to seal over by leaving out undisturbed for a couple of days.

Gardeners in zones 9–12 can grow ginger directly in the ground as a perennial. Plant each section horizontally with eyes facing up in rich soil about 4 inches deep and 12 inches apart. Because ginger needs a moist environment, a thick layer of mulch is helpful. Throughout a long summer, thin, green, strappy leaves grow, making a very pretty and ornamental plant in the garden.

Gardeners in temperate climates can try growing ginger in pots or as annuals. Rhizomes grow horizontally

chinese culinary ginger relatives

Zingiber mioga, also known as Japanese myoga ginger, is a woodland perennial that is hardy to 0 degrees Fahrenheit. It yellows in the fall and becomes dormant in the winter. This relative of common Chinese ginger is grown for its edible flower buds, which are mildly spicy and thinly sliced or shredded and used to flavor soups. The buds are also tempura-fried or pickled.

Another rhizome related to ginger is *Alpinia galanga* or Thai galangal. Although it is a knotty rhizome like common ginger, Asian cooks and connoisseurs would not use them interchangeably. Galangal is a fragrant rhizome popular in Indonesian, Vietnamese, and Thai cuisines. It is an important ingredient in the Thai tom yum soup.

but do send down roots, so use a pot that is wide but also has some depth. For one or two rhizomes, a pot 12 inches deep and wide would be sufficient. Start rhizomes inside in pots in early spring and then bring them outdoors as the weather warms. Replant into larger pots if the plants seems to outgrow their containers. In the fall, when temperatures drop to about 50 degrees Fahrenheit, growth will begin to slow; at this point bring the pots indoors and place them in front of a sunny south-facing window. With its long sturdy leaves, ginger makes an attractive houseplant as the gardener waits for the plant to mature and leaves to die back.

Whether grown in the ground or in containers, ginger will be large enough for harvesting in the fall after 8–10 months of healthy growth when tops begin to dry out. To harvest, carefully dig up the ginger rhizomes. They will have grown and lengthened on the ends. Use what you need, making sure to save some of the rhizomes to replant for your next harvest. Gardeners in zones 9–12 can replant immediately. Gardeners in zones with cold winters can try storing the rhizomes in some damp sand through the winter, or just start new ginger plants in the spring with new rhizomes. Alternatively, some gardeners keep ginger going year round in medium-sized pots of soil or sand. When you want a piece, you can unbury part of the root, cut off a knob, and return it to the soil.

GINGER FISH CONGEE

Congee can be eaten plain—perhaps topped with your choice of crumbled salted duck egg, crispy fried shallots, or dried shredded pork—or just seasoned with salt. Sometimes, congee is stepped up with the addition of fish fillets as in this recipe. When making congee, it's important to stir frequently to ensure the rice does not scorch. As the grains continue to break down and the congee begins to thicken, add water as necessary to create the consistency you like. A reasonable ideal is to aim for the consistency of thin chowder.

SERVES 6

1 tablespoon Shaoxing rice wine

1 tablespoon dark (toasted) sesame oil, plus more for serving

1 tablespoon light soy sauce

1 teaspoon finely minced ginger, plus 1 (1-inch) section of ginger, peeled and finely julienned

Dash of white pepper

¾ pound flounder or sole fillets, sliced on diagonal into very thin slices about ¼ inch thin

14 cups water

1 cup jasmine rice (or other long grain rice), soaked in water for 1 hour

Salt

Cilantro, coarsely chopped to garnish

1. Combine the wine, sesame oil, soy sauce, minced ginger, and pepper in a medium bowl. Add the fish slices and marinate for 30 minutes at room temperature.

2. Bring the water to a boil over high heat in a stockpot. Drain the presoaked rice and add it to the pot. Boil on high for about 30 minutes, stirring frequently. Be especially watchful near the end of the cooking time, adding about a half cup of water at a time if the congee becomes too thick. The congee is ready when the grains have completely broken down and look like they've exploded. Be careful of burning-hot splatters while cooking. After the congee is cooked, salt generously to taste.

3. Add the marinated fish and julienned ginger to the pot. Stir gently until the fish is cooked through, 2–3 minutes. Ladle into bowls and serve with a thin drizzle of sesame oil and chopped cilantro.

IN THE KITCHEN In Chinese cuisine, ginger is infused into just about every dish, giving food its distinctive Asian bite. It's made into candy, tea, and soda. It livens up stir-fries and soups. It can be crushed, grated, minced, chopped, julienned, sliced, pickled, candied, and steeped.

If my mom is making a stir-fry, she'll usually slice a few pieces of ginger, unpeeled, and add it to some hot oil with a few garlic cloves crushed with the flat side of a knife. This cooking process, called *bao wok*, releases the fragrance of the ginger and garlic and flavors the oil. One swirl of this flavored oil around the wok, and she's prepared to add the rest of the ingredients. When the ginger slices are used for flavor in this way and not for eating, you don't need to peel them.

If the ginger will be eaten, I prefer to peel it first. Despite the knots and curves of the root, you can easily scrap the skin off ginger with the edge of a spoon. After harvesting a hunk of ginger, if you can't use it all, cut into chunks, wrap carefully, and store in the freezer until needed.

New shoots and young rhizomes may be purple and smooth, unlike the yellow ginger found in the supermarket. While this ginger is tender, it has a very subtle flavor. This young ginger is suited for marinating foods, and is not commonly used in Chinese cuisine. Mature, yellow ginger is preferred because it is more flavorful and can stand up in a stir-fry with stronger spices.

Sometimes, a mature piece of ginger can be tough or stringy, and unpleasant to eat. In this case, slice and pound the ginger a bit and cook with it. Before serving, remove the ginger pieces. Another idea is to grate the ginger and then squeeze the grated ginger for juice to flavor sauces. This is a smart way to add ginger flavor to peanut sauce while still maintaining a smooth texture.

Cucurbita maxima

kabocha

南瓜

MANDARIN *nán'guā*
CANTONESE *naam gwaa*

Kabocha, also known as Japanese or Chinese pumpkin, is a beautiful, dark green, striped or mottled squash with yellow or orange flesh, depending on maturity. Weighing anywhere from 2 to 5 pounds, this slightly flattened squash is smaller than the average field pumpkin. I like kabocha for its sweeter, nuttier taste. 'Delica' and the yellow-orange 'Kurinishiki' are both highly productive types with great flavor. The dry texture of this squash makes it an excellent multipurpose choice for cooking and baking. Kabocha is high in beta-carotene, iron, vitamin C, and potassium. For its health benefits, manageable size, and numerous uses, kabocha is a wonderful plant to add to your garden.

IN THE GARDEN Kabocha requires about 100 days to mature. In late spring or early summer, when the danger of frost has passed and soil begins to warm, plant one or two kabocha seeds 1 inch deep in hills 4–6 feet apart where they can be left to ramble. Kabocha requires consistent moisture and plants may need to be watered every day during the hottest part of the summer. A thick layer of mulch may help to conserve water, and the large leaves from the plant will help keep roots cool as well.

You can eat kabocha when it is small and has yellow flesh, but for best flavor, leave squash growing on the vine until the skin toughens and looks less glossy. A mature kabocha will be a mellow orange inside, deeper in color than a young squash. This ideal time to harvest kabocha is when the vines begin to die back, about 100 days after germination. Be sure to harvest all the pumpkins before the first frost. Simply cut the squash off the vine leaving 1–2 inches of the slightly dried-out stem attached.

The process of curing is important to achieve the sweet, smooth taste of a kabocha at its best. After cutting off the vine, leave kabocha out to cure in the sun or another warm place for 2 weeks. If curing outdoors and there is danger of an overnight frost, be sure to cover with a blanket (or bring

The great taste of dry, firm kabocha works well in any recipe that calls for pumpkin or most winter squashes.

Sankaya, a Thai dessert made of steamed kabocha and custard, is as delicious as it is elegant.

inside). During the first 2 weeks, some of the starch in the pumpkin converts to sugar. After this period, store in a cool place for about a month. If cured properly, the sweetness will develop and the skin will harden a bit, extending the period of time it stays fresh. You can store bruise-free and uncut kabocha in a cool place for months. Kabocha reaches its prime taste and texture about 1½ months after it is harvested.

IN THE KITCHEN The firm, dry texture of kabocha means it is excellent pureed, baked, sautéed, roasted, steamed, or fried. Kabocha works well in both sweet and savory dishes, and can be substituted for pumpkin and most winter squashes including butternut. Chinese cooks love using the nutritious squash in soups, stews, or alongside other substantial vegetables or meat.

Aside from these home-style meals, kabocha is used in desserts such as a delicious fall pie, a flavorful ice cream, and a Thai dessert called sankaya. To make sankaya, custard is poured into the hollowed-out squash, which is then steamed whole for nearly an hour to soften the edible skin and then cut into beautiful bi-colored slices to serve.

KABOCHA WITH GROUND PORK IN
BLACK BEAN SAUCE

This is a hearty and harmonious dish with just the right balance of sweet and savory. For a vegetarian option, prepare the kabocha with a few meaty shiitake mushrooms instead of the pork.

SERVES 4

2   teaspoons cornstarch

2   teaspoons soy sauce

½   teaspoon sugar

1   teaspoon dark (toasted) sesame oil

Pinch of white pepper

½   pound ground pork

1   small (about 2-pound) kabocha

1   teaspoon minced garlic

1   tablespoon fermented black beans, rinsed, drained, and coarsely chopped

2–3 tablespoons corn or peanut oil

4   cilantro sprigs, chopped for garnish

1. Stir 1 teaspoon of the cornstarch into ½ cup water. Set aside.

2. Combine the soy sauce, sugar, remaining 1 teaspoon cornstarch, sesame oil, and white pepper in a bowl. Add the pork and marinate for about 20 minutes at room temperature.

3. Prepare kabocha like other hard squash or pumpkins. I like to split the kabocha in half, remove seeds, cut into wedges, and then cut off the rind. Cut kabocha into large bite-sized chunks.

4. Heat a wok over medium-high heat and then add 2 tablespoons of the oil. When hot, add the pork, stirring until cooked. Remove and set aside.

5. Add the remaining 1 tablespoon oil to the wok and when hot, add the garlic and black beans and stir-fry until fragrant, 1 minute. Add the kabocha and stir, then add ½ cup water. Reduce heat to a simmer, cover, and cook, stirring occasionally until the kabocha is soft, 8–10 minutes, adding more water if necessary.

6. Add the ground pork and cornstarch solution. When the sauce bubbles and thickens, remove it from the heat. Garnish with chopped cilantro and serve.

Brassica juncea

mustard greens

MANDARIN *jiècài*
CANTONESE *gai choy*

芥菜

Mustard greens are grown all over the world and come in many forms with leaves that are flat or curly, feathery or smooth, and in varying shades of green and red. The most common Chinese mustards are attractive semi-heading vegetables with thick, broad leaves that curl inward. It's easy to identify Chinese mustard among the other Asian greens by looking at the base of the plant where the wide pale green stems curve tightly around the heart. The darker green leaves loosen as they reach the top of the plant.

With each specific look comes just as many nuances in taste from a pungent horseradish-like flavor to a milder taste similar to chard. The popular 'Bau Sin' is particularly mild and sweet, and requires only about 45 days to maturity. Chinese mustard greens are typically not as strong in taste as their Western counterparts, but are just as packed with iron and vitamins A, C, E, and K. Nutritionists value mustard greens for their anti-inflammatory and cholesterol-lowering abilities. Mustard greens have also been found to be high in a phytonutrient that may have cancer-preventing qualities.

IN THE GARDEN Mustard greens are easy to grow in virtually any type of soil. They do tend to bolt quickly when the weather gets hot in late spring and early summer, so fall is a good time to plant. Mustard greens are also milder in flavor when grown in cooler weather. About 60 days before first frost, sow seeds directly, 1/4 inch deep, in a sunny or partially shady spot in the garden. Thin to 10–12 inches apart. Chinese mustard is a slow grower but you can begin harvesting leaves when they are only a few inches tall and then at any stage. Pungency increases with maturity.

If growing a spring crop, harvest mustard greens before they bolt. Because plants may bolt before they've had a chance to be cut and grow again, it's a good idea to plant successively to help extend the spring harvest season. Mustards enjoy the cool weather of spring and the flavor

Chinese mustards have a characteristic look with tightly curved stems at the base of the plants.

of the leaves can become bitter and tough during periods of heat or drought.

Chinese mustard greens are sometimes used as a green manure by sowing seeds in fallow areas of the garden. When plants have grown, they're cut and left in place as mulch. Then, prior to planting a new crop, the dried plants are worked into the soil. Another bonus: some evidence exists that as the mustard breaks down, it releases a chemical that prevents root rot in pea plants.

IN THE KITCHEN Mustard is versatile in the kitchen, as different varieties have varying levels of heat. It can be mild and slightly peppery or hot and almost bitter. Some people eat it raw—chopped or shredded and added to green salads—but it is most often cooked first, which tends to tame the flavor somewhat. You can use Chinese mustard as a substitute in recipes that call for chard or spinach. It also works well in a light chicken soup for a little spicy kick, stir-fried along with other vegetables, or steamed as a side dish. To preserve the many nutrients found in mustard greens, do not overcook. In China, the fleshier-stemmed mustard greens are often pickled whole (or chopped and pickled) as a tart and spicy condiment.

Brassica rapa Pekinensis Group

napa cabbage

MANDARIN *dàbái cài*
CANTONESE *daai bok choy*

大白菜

Napa cabbages are tall, cylindrical heading cabbages with a mild, delicate flavor and high water content. The outer leaves, which are typically not eaten, are sturdy and similar to those of the round European *Brassica oleracea* cabbage. The inner leaves are more tender, crisp, and less fibrous than their Western counterparts. This popular vegetable is chunky and barrel-shaped, with tightly packed, deeply crinkled leaves and thick white ribs. It is well known in North America as Napa cabbage, either after the Japanese word for cabbage, *nappa*, or because it was first commercially cultivated in California's Napa Valley region. What *is* certain is that Chinese farmers have been growing this delicious, versatile, and nutritious vegetable for thousands of years.

Napa cabbages are high in vitamins C and K, and contain folates, dietary fiber, and many types of antioxidants. All this makes it an extremely healthful, great tasting, easy-to-use vegetable that is nearly calorie-free.

IN THE GARDEN Napa cabbage is a cool-weather biennial plant typically grown as an annual. It thrives in temperatures of 60–70 degrees Fahrenheit; cold snaps or hot days (above 75 degrees Fahrenheit) can cause the plant to bolt. Although some gardeners may have success with growing in the spring, Napa cabbage requires 50–85 cool days to harvest. Hot weather often catches spring cabbage plants unaware and causes bolting. My friends who have tried Napa cabbage in the spring have also had serious issues with pests such as slugs, flea beetles, and some cabbage worms. We usually have a better Napa cabbage harvest when we sow cabbages in the early fall, about 10 weeks before first frost.

Plant seeds in rows about 1/2 inch deep. When seedlings are a few inches high, thin to about 18 inches apart. The thinnings can be carefully dug out and transplanted or simply used in a salad or stir-fry. Napa cabbages have shallow root systems so cultivate carefully and keep the cabbage rows

Napa cabbage is a crisp vegetable with delicate flavor that is traditionally used to make Korean kimchi. It is delicious in salads and is a great substitute for recipes that call for lettuce or cabbage.

'michihili' chinese cabbage

'Michihili', another popular type of Chinese cabbage, grows to about 15 inches tall, with stark white ribs and darker green, soft, leafy tops. The base is tight like Napa cabbage and it is just as easy to grow and has a similar taste. The difference is that the leafy tops are generally looser and softer and can be eaten like romaine lettuce.

well-watered in order to grow sturdy, tall cabbages with tightly formed heads.

Napa cabbages are ready for harvesting when they're about 12 inches high and when you can feel a firm and formed heart when you squeeze the top. When mature, fall-planted cabbage can tolerate cold weather and some light frosts. Though it will slow or stop growing, the fall-planted Napa cabbage can sit waiting for you in the winter garden until ready for use. Peel any tough or frost-damaged outer leaves and use the sweet and tender heart of the cabbage. Store harvested Napa cabbage in a cold shed, garage, or basement for up to 2 or 3 months.

IN THE KITCHEN Growing up, my father and his family used Napa cabbage year round in dozens of dishes due to its great flavor, refreshing crispness, and versatility. Of all the Chinese leafy vegetables, Napa cabbage is among my first choices for recipes that call for uncooked greens. Unlike European cabbages, which can be difficult to digest, the mild Napa cabbage is a great choice for salads. One of my favorite American bistros makes a salad I've been enjoying for years with chunks of sirloin steak, long Asian noodles, shredded Napa cabbage, mango, and a sweet and spicy dressing. Napa cabbage is an excellent light meal when shredded, combined with other favorite ingredients, and rolled in a rice paper spring roll wrapper alongside a homemade dipping sauce.

Napa cabbage is great stir-fried or steamed and then seasoned with a sauce. Because the leaves are thinner and more delicate than some of the sturdier Asian greens, a shorter cooking time does the trick. Harvested in late fall, Napa cabbage is also a wonderful addition to soups on a cold day. I grew up eating a clear bone broth soup flavored with dried shrimp, cellophane noodles, and Napa cabbage.

what are those tiny black spots?

Harmless, tiny black spots may appear on the ribs of the plant, especially toward the heart of the cabbage. This physical disorder, sometimes called black speck or pepper spot, may be caused by a few factors: low temperatures in the garden followed by warmer temperatures during storage, high rates of fertilizer, and harvesting when overly mature. These black spots are more of a problem with commercially grown Napa cabbage, as home gardeners can cut a head of cabbage at the prime time for harvesting and bring it directly to the kitchen.

In our family, what we enjoy most is my father's fall dumplings made with lump crabmeat, pork, and Napa cabbage. The cabbage's high water content helps create a juicy filling.

Napa cabbage is also the primary vegetable used in Korean kimchi and is great for many pickle recipes. Aside from the culinary uses in Asia, Napa cabbage has a mild taste that would be an easy substitution for non-Asian recipes that call for cabbage or lettuce, such as in coleslaw.

To use, cut like you would any heading lettuce or cabbage according to your recipe. Dirt can sometimes get trapped in the very wrinkled leaves, but because the cabbage grows with leaves so tightly furled, the center of the Napa cabbage is generally pristine.

CRAB, PORK, AND NAPA CABBAGE DUMPLINGS

My father makes dumplings throughout the year, usually taking requests for the different filling combinations, both traditional and of his own creation. I am finally revealing a family secret with the recording of my father's crab, pork, and Napa cabbage dumpling recipe. Because Napa cabbage is so mild in taste, its presence is barely noticeable, but the high water content of the cabbage contributes to the juiciness of these dumplings. You can purchase dumpling wrappers in Asian supermarkets.

MAKES AT LEAST 24 DUMPLINGS

- ⅓ cup finely chopped cilantro
- 1 pound Napa cabbage, chopped fine with excess water drained and squeezed out
- 3 spring onions, chopped very fine
- 1 inch ginger, minced
- ¼ pound crabmeat, picked through and chopped
- 1 pound ground pork, finely minced
- 1 tablespoon Shaoxing rice wine or brandy
- ¼ cup soy sauce
- 2 tablespoons corn or vegetable oil
- ¼ cup dark (toasted) sesame oil
- 2 teaspoons sweet bean sauce
- Pinch of sugar
- Pinch of salt
- Pinch of white pepper
- 1 (30-count or more) package of round white dumpling wrappers
- Soy sauce or black vinegar for serving

1. Combine the cilantro, Napa cabbage, spring onions, ginger, crabmeat, ground pork, rice wine, soy sauce, corn oil, sesame oil, sweet bean sauce, sugar, salt, white pepper, and ½ cup of water in a large bowl. Stir vigorously for several minutes—this laborious step is the key to creating a filling with a light texture.

2. With a dumpling wrapper in the palm of one hand, place about a tablespoon of filling in the center of the wrapper. Bring the sides together, pleating as necessary and forming a little purse. Gently cup the filled center in your hands so it does not get crushed and squeeze the edges together tightly with both hands. Continue to fill all dumpling wrappers.

3. Fill a wok or deep pan with water to 2 inches below the top. Heat water to a rolling boil. Working in batches so the wok is not too crowded, drop dumplings in and continuously and gently stir until they float to the top. At this point, add ½–1 cup of cold water to bring the boil down. When water comes back up to a boil, add another ½–1 cup of water. This process allows dumplings to cook gently without breaking. When the water comes back up to a boil again, dumplings should be another minute or so away from being ready.

4. Test for doneness by pressing into the dumpling. The filling inside should feel firm and be very juicy but cooked through and hot. Serve with a little soy sauce or black vinegar.

Like most cooks who make dumplings by hand, my father doesn't follow a written recipe for the dumpling wrappers, but rather is guided by the texture of the dough and his years of experience. He separates the dough into little round pieces, flattens them, and rolls them out. The process is skillful and speedy—one hand moves the streamlined rolling pin while the other turns the wrapper around and around until it is consistently thin and ready to fill.

Raphanus sativus

radish

MANDARIN *bái luóbo*
CANTONESE *loh bok*

白
蘿
蔔

蘿
蔔

One day, I asked my father about radishes he used to grow and he went into a reverie about the rows and rows of radishes in his garden in China. After harvesting, he would cut off the leafy tops and bury the radishes in pits outside, under dirt and then later, snow, for storage. He talked about the hot flavor that becomes frost-sweetened in the late fall and early winter. Crunching into the radish, you'd be met with the initial bite, but beyond that first taste, the radishes were so juicy and sweet that they earned the nickname "radish sweeter than pear" and were sometimes called winter pears.

Anyone who likes the small, round European radish will love the Chinese radish. Chinese radishes are similar to their Western counterparts in their crisp texture and pungent hot flavor. However, while radishes available in North American supermarkets are small, red, and round, Chinese radishes are usually white, elongated, and gigantic: about 12 inches long and weighing up to a few pounds per radish.

The most well-known radishes in Asian cuisine are commonly known by

Daikon radish has a slightly hot flavor and is excellent pickled.

trash can radishes

Consider growing Chinese radishes in a tall, clean, trash can with many holes drilled in the sides and bottom. You may find this method results in long healthy radishes that are even more beautiful than those grown in a raised bed with deeply augmented soil.

their Japanese name, daikon, or their Hindi name, mooli. Radishes grown more locally in China look similar to the daikon radish but are light green near the top few inches of the radish, close to the leaves. These Chinese radishes are called *loh bak* in Cantonese. Some people believe they're sweeter than the daikon, some feel they're hotter. I remember a story my mom told me of her childhood in Northern Shandong, a region with frigid winters. One way she and her siblings staved off the cold was to take bites of Chinese radishes, which would warm them from the inside. What the children didn't know was that the radishes were good for them too, being high in vitamin C and calcium.

There are many varieties of Chinese radishes, each with specific shapes, colors, tastes, and names. In addition to the long white daikon, and the "green meat" radishes that my father grew in Shandong, is a beautiful, sweet-hot, red variety called 'Red Meat' or 'Beauty Heart', referring to the red color in the center of the radish. This variety is smaller, rounder, and stunning when sliced and added to salads.

IN THE GARDEN All types of radishes are extremely easy to grow, germinating quickly for a spring or fall to winter harvest. Because Chinese radishes can grow to 12 inches or longer, loosen the soil as much as possible for best results. Whereas smaller radishes can be tucked between crops, Chinese radishes do better in an open site with room to grow, not shaded or crowded by taller plants.

Most radish varieties are cool-weather types and sowing seeds directly in the garden in late summer yields the best results for a fall harvest. I like the protection from extreme weather that fall planting provides. Radishes tolerate frost well and when planted in the fall, are also safe from a sudden heat wave that might cause a spring crop to prematurely flower, making radishes hotter and tougher. Radishes also need consistent moisture while growing and fall offers an ideal environment. Fall radishes can be left in the ground for a little while after maturity, so long as it doesn't get too cold, although they can sometimes become pithy or woody and unpleasantly pungent if left too long.

Sow seeds about ½ inch deep and 4–10 inches apart, depending on the variety. Space rows 12 inches apart so radish leaves have room to stretch out as they grow to be tall and sturdy. After harvesting, store radishes in a cold and humid place or in the refrigerator. If you have harvested more than you can use, try cutting them into ¼ inch slices and dehydrating in a food dehydrator.

Spring planting is another option. If doing so, consider starting seeds indoors in very early spring. While it may seem a tedious chore to transplant a row of radishes, remember that these radishes grow very large and just one radish can be enough to feed a family. Harvest spring radishes as soon as they are mature because they can become spongy if left in the ground too long and they will bolt in the heat. If spring sowing, consider a slow-to-bolt variety such as the daikon radish 'Tokinashi'.

IN THE KITCHEN Like many Chinese vegetables, all parts of the radish are edible, from the young foliage to the root, seeds, and seedpods. Most often, people grow radishes for their crisp, juicy, and zingy root. Chinese radishes can be pickled, stewed, or stir-fried.

Pickled or marinated radishes are a delicious sweet, sour, or spicy condiment, and are a regular feature in the small side dishes of Korean *banchan*. They are also julienned and made into the spicy and sour carrot and daikon pickle that completes a Vietnamese *banh mi* sandwich. Because Chinese radishes have a high water content, they are usually cut into pieces and salted to remove excess water before using.

Depending on the recipe, radishes can be sliced, cut into chunks, julienned, or shredded. They are also grated and eaten raw in a number of different sauces. One of my favorite simple meals on the menu of Japanese restaurants is a dish of cold soba noodles that is usually served with

Green radishes were more commonly grown in the region my parents grew up in.

cover crop radishes

Daikon radishes are known for being able to improve a garden's soil and are sometimes grown not for food, but as a cover crop. They are quick growing, shade out weeds, and send down strong roots that break up compacted soil. Their long taproots scavenge for nutrients deep in the ground and bring them closer to the surface of the soil. In cold climates, several freezing days will kill the plants, requiring little work to benefit from this effective cover crop. In warmer zones without killing freezes, radishes can be mowed in late fall. By spring, the roots will have decomposed, leaving aerated soil that warms and dries out more quickly for spring planting.

a small bowl of a mild dipping sauce with neat little piles of wasabi, thinly sliced scallions, grated radish, and other condiments to flavor the sauce. Just before each bite, you dip the soba into the sauce and eat it.

Radishes are a great vegetable to have on hand in the fall and winter. Though they contain some heat, radishes also pick up the flavors of other food ingredients. As such, they can be interesting substitutions for potatoes, turnips, carrots, or parsnips. And because they have a beautiful white color and are so large, artistic chefs love to carve them into objects such as elaborate flowers to garnish serving platters.

Lactuca sativa var. *asparagina*

stem lettuce

萵
筍

MANDARIN *wōsǔn*
CANTONESE *woh seon*

Stem lettuce might be the most unusual looking of all the leafy lettuces. It looks like an arrangement of romaine or iceberg lettuce leaves atop a tall fat stem. Though the soft green leaves can get bitter as the plant matures, they are delicious and mild when young. However, stem lettuce is not grown specifically for the edible leaves, but rather for the thick, crisp stem, which tapers slightly toward the top and holds up the cluster of loose leaves.

Also commonly known as celtuce, stem lettuce is not a cross between celery and lettuce as the name might suggest, though many do describe the taste of the coveted stems as similar to celery, lettuce, asparagus, or cucumbers. The crisp texture and mild flavor of stem lettuce is enjoyed—raw or cooked—in a wide variety of dishes, and it is high in vitamin C and potassium.

IN THE GARDEN Cold-tolerant stem lettuce is an excellent fall crop and germinates best in cool soil, around 60 degrees Fahrenheit. Sow seeds directly in the garden in late summer (or mid-spring for a spring crop).

Although the leafy tops of stem lettuce are edible, this vegetable is primarily grown for its thick, crisp stems.

Slice, shred, or julienne the stems and enjoy them raw or cooked.

When baby plants stand about 3 inches tall, thin to about 12 inches apart. Because roots are situated fairly close to the surface it's helpful to mulch rows to keep weeds at bay and prevent damage done while cultivating the lettuce.

When plants have a top of several leaves and stems are about an inch thick, harvest the leafy greens by pulling off a few lower leaves from around the stem. Harvesting just the lower leaves in the early stages stimulates the growth of the plant and encourages a thicker stem to form. When the stems grow to about 12 inches tall and a few inches thick, you can harvest the entire plant in order to eat the crisp stem as a vegetable. Though stem lettuce is tolerant of both cold and heat, the plant may bolt if the weather becomes too hot. 'Summer 38' is a cultivar known to be resistant to bolting due to heat and is a good one to try for fall and spring crops.

IN THE KITCHEN To prepare the stems, cut off the leafy tops. Peel the bitter outer skin with a vegetable peeler, and then slice, shred, or julienne the tender translucent green heart. Try pickling the stems, or eat them raw in salads or as part of a cold vegetable platter (they are a great alternative to other crisp vegetables such as celery or cucumber). The stem pieces also retain some of their crunchy texture when cooked. Stir-fry julienned pieces with hot peppers and garlic, marinated chicken or pork, or other vegetables. In Sichuan, where stem lettuce is a popular vegetable, it is used as cooks in other parts of China might use bamboo shoots.

As long as they're not too bitter for your taste, try the leafy green tops raw in salads, or quickly sauté them with some minced or slivered garlic and then season with soy sauce or oyster sauce.

Colocasia esculenta

taro root

MANDARIN *yùtou*
CANTONESE *wu tao*

芋頭

The tall and attractive *Colocasia esculenta* is a perennial tropical or subtropical plant often known by its common name, elephant ear. Buried underground at the roots of the long sturdy stems are the edible, brown, hairy, rough-looking, fist-sized corms. When peeled, the corms display an interior color of purple (as in the violet-stemmed version), white, or off-white. Although the stems and leaves are also edible, the corms, usually referred to as taro root, are the most commonly eaten part.

Mild tasting with a starchy texture, taro root can be transformed into a variety of sweet and savory foods. I grew up on the small football-shaped fried taro dumplings in dim sum restaurants, have treated myself to buttery pastries with a sweet taro filling, and have sipped on taro-flavored bubble tea on many summer afternoons. Unbeknownst to me, I even tasted a variety of taro root in St. Lucia, where it is called dasheen. In Hawaii, mashed taro is made into poi,

Taro root (small taro corms) is made into many different foods from thin salted chips to birthday cakes to savory dim sum dishes.

taro: toxic when raw

Keep in mind no part of the taro plant should be eaten raw, and all parts must be cooked first. Not only would the leaves, stems, and corms not taste good, but all parts of the plant release calcium oxalate crystals which can be toxic.

an important cultural food. Poi is generally allowed to ferment, which adds additional health benefits.

Taro is comparable in calories to starchy tubers such as potatoes or sweet potatoes. Eaten in moderation, the corms are a good-for-you carbohydrate, especially when steamed or boiled. Taro is high in dietary fiber and contains antioxidants and vitamins A, B6, C, and E. Taro leaves also contain high levels of beta-carotene. That makes taro a delicious and versatile ingredient to experiment with; one that is good for digestion, eyes, skin, and the immune system.

IN THE GARDEN Taro plants require a tropical or subtropical climate in order to produce edible corms. Plants do well in the warm to hot temperatures of zones 8–11 and require 4–6 months of 75-degree days in order to produce a reasonable harvest. Taro plants also love moist growing conditions as they are indigenous to swampy areas by streams and in rainforests. Aside from this ideal growing environment, some people have successfully grown taro in water or bog gardens. Gardeners in milder zones can experiment with growing in very large containers or extending the season by growing in a greenhouse.

Plant taro corms in the early spring for a late summer harvest, or in early summer for a late fall harvest. The best way to start taro plants is by finding a few healthy corms in the produce aisle of Asian supermarkets. They will usually sprout readily. Plant tubers 6–8 inches deep, and be sure to provide consistent moisture throughout the season. This may sometimes require watering twice a day. One idea may be to grow taro in a trench. Another idea is to create a flooded area by sinking in a few plastic jugs with the tops cut off and holes poked in them in a ring surrounding the taro, leaving about 12 inches of space around the taro plant. Keep the jugs filled with water to create a

Ground shrimp and pork are shaped into patties, pressed into shredded taro, and fried crisp in this favorite dim sum plate.

consistently moist environment for the taro.

After a long hot growing season the leaves may begin to yellow and die away. At this point, check for a harvest by carefully digging up the plant with a garden fork. Depending on your climate, corms may be harvested while leaves are still lush and green. After unearthing the corms, separate, carefully wash, and then cure them in the sun for a few days. Be sure to save some corms to replant. Either replant the whole corm, or try cutting off the top inch of a corm containing a growing eye, allowing the cut to dry out for a day, and then replanting.

IN THE KITCHEN Although the corms are the most commonly eaten part, the sturdy leaves of the taro plant are also edible when cooked. Steam or boil the leaves for a good 45 minutes or so until they become tender and then stir-fry them or add to other recipes like you would any other cooked leafy green. The cooked leaves can also be used to wrap foods. As a green vegetable, taro leaves are sometimes described as similar to cabbage and contain high levels of beta-carotene.

Taro root has extremely versatile culinary uses: I've seen it in drinks, soups, stir-fries, and desserts. In sweet treats, I tend to associate taro with coconut as they complement each other and are often paired together. In savory foods, taro is used similarly to a potato and can be cooked in as many ways: boiled, steamed, fried, or mashed. I like taro sliced with a mandolin and deep-fried like chips, or filled with meat and shrimp, shaped into dumplings, and

TARO WITH COCONUT MILK AND TAPIOCA

My Chinese relatives tend to turn up their noses at most Western desserts, complaining that they're too sweet. A comforting, just-sweet-enough dessert like this one is satisfying at the end of a big Chinese meal, especially when it is served warm. Tapioca pearls are sold in Asian supermarkets in sizes ranging from the bean-sized pearls (used to make popular bubble teas) to the smallest pearls, which are called for in this dessert.

SERVES 4

2 cups peeled, diced taro root

½ cup small (2- to 3-millimeter) tapioca pearls

10 cups water

1 (13.5-ounce) can unsweetened coconut milk

½ cup rock sugar

1. Place taro root in a medium pot and add about 6 cups of the water, or enough to cover the taro root by 2 inches. Bring to a boil and then reduce heat to simmer until the taro is soft, about 20 minutes.

2. Meanwhile, bring the remaining 4 cups water to a boil in a large saucepan. Slowly add the tapioca while stirring to prevent sticking. Boil for 10 minutes and then remove from heat. Cover tightly and let sit for 15–25 more minutes, or until tapioca pearls are clear inside. Drain in a sieve and run cold water over the tapioca.

3. When taro root is soft, drain and remove about one-third of the taro root. Return the rest to the pot and mash with a potato masher. Over low heat, stir the coconut milk into the mashed taro. Add the sugar and simmer over low-medium heat until the sugar dissolves. Add the reserved chunks of taro root and drained tapioca. Serve warm or chilled.

fried as they are at dim sum restaurants. When I was young, I remember Chinese banquet dinners with elegant taro presentations. The taro was shredded and then formed into a bowl-sized "bird's nest" basket and deep-fried to hold its shape. The nest would then be filled with an equally impressive stir-fry dish. Because taro tends to pick up the flavors of the other foods it is cooked with, it goes well with just about any dish and can be an unexpected substitution in recipes that call for potatoes, carrots, turnips, or just about any other starchy root vegetable.

giant taro

My Asian supermarket sells two types of taro: tennis ball–sized *Colocasia esculenta* and *Alocasia macrorrhiza*, often called giant taro. The latter looks like a fat, foot-long cassava root, but has more clearly defined segments on its outer brown peel. It tastes similar to the smaller taro, delicious and starchy, and also needs to be cooked before eating to remove toxins. Giant taro requires a large space—it will grow up to 15 feet tall and almost as wide with 3- to 6-foot-long leaves—and plants can take up to two years to produce a large corm. For these reasons I don't recommend that home gardeners plant giant taro as a food crop, but it could be a fun way to add a tropical feel to your landscape.

Giant taro (in the foreground and on the right) is too big for most gardeners to grow as a food crop.

Brassica rapa Chinensis Group

tatsoi

烏
塌
菜

MANDARIN *wū tā cài*
CANTONESE *wu taap choy*

Most commonly known by its Japanese name tatsoi, this bok choy relative is also called flat cabbage (describing its prostrate appearance) or rosette bok choy (describing the neat concentric circles formed by the round dark green leaves). Chinese connoisseurs enjoy tatsoi for its beauty as much as its taste, and many know it as *tai koo choy*, which means ancient vegetable.

Tatsoi has a mild mustard taste and is sturdier as well as more nutritious than regular bok choy. Traditional Chinese medicine practitioners use tatsoi to strengthen the liver, blood, and bones. Tatsoi has high levels of calcium, vitamins A and C, and folates. In fact, this superfood has almost twice the vitamin C of a serving of orange juice, and tops the list of calcium-rich cruciferous vegetables.

Tatsoi lights up the landscape of my father's fall vegetable garden when most vegetables are done for the year. He loves both the taste and texture and looks forward to that first frost to hit the tatsoi and sweeten the leaves.

IN THE GARDEN Tatsoi is a cool-weather crop and is grown just like bok choy. A productive spring crop may be difficult to maintain because plants will go to seed when the heat of summer arrives; flea beetles can also be a nuisance when spring sown. A fall crop stands up better to pests and bolting.

Tatsoi is a slow-growing but carefree vegetable with a long harvest period. A fall crop actually extends from fall through winter in colder climates. Tatsoi has been known to withstand temperatures as low as 15 degrees Fahrenheit. It is not uncommon to make a quick trip to the garden in parka and gloves to harvest tatsoi from under snow cover.

For a successful fall crop, sow seeds directly in the ground in late summer or early fall. Plant about ¼ inch deep, in rows 18–24 inches apart. As plants grow, thin tatsoi to about 8 inches apart. Keep the soil moist as the tatsoi germinates and

When hit with frost, the leaves of tatsoi gain a hint of sweetness.

When it gets cold, leaves hover closer to the ground, giving tatsoi its characteristic look and nickname of flat cabbage.

grows. Plants grow upright in warmer weather but as the temperatures drop, tatsoi becomes more prone. It takes 6–8 weeks to mature fully; baby leaves are ready after only 20–25 days. To harvest, cut the entire rosette or cut outer leaves as needed.

IN THE KITCHEN Because tatsoi grows so close to the ground, it is important to rinse the leaves well to remove dirt and grit. Eat baby tatsoi leaves raw in salads or add them to salad mixes that will highlight their mild mustard taste and tender texture. They are also excellent tossed with a tangy dressing and wilted slightly. You can cook mature tatsoi either as separate leaves or as a whole rosette. These versatile and healthful greens are delicious in soups, stir-fries, or simply sautéed (my family's preference). Tatsoi works well as a substitution for any Asian leafy green, spinach, chard, or cabbage.

Eleocharis dulcis

water chestnut

荸
薺

馬
蹄

MANDARIN *bíqí*
CANTONESE *ma tai*

Lucky is the gardener with a long season and established water garden, for the water chestnut is an attractive tender perennial that anchors any water garden with its spiky grass-like foliage. It also produces edible corms at the end of the season. Before I tasted a fresh water chestnut—mud rinsed off, patted dry, peeled, and sliced right before eating—I thought I hated water chestnuts based on my experience with canned water chestnuts at Chinese restaurants with their wet and semi-crunchy texture and bland flavor. Though often used as an addition to a typical chicken, vegetable, and brown sauce dish, I prefer to play up the slightly sweet and nutty flavor in a dessert or snack just by itself.

Traditional Chinese medicine practitioners have tapped into the health benefits of water chestnuts for generations. The outsides of the corms are crushed for anti-inflammatory and antimicrobial uses; the inside of the water chestnut can be ground, juiced, steeped in wine, or just sliced and eaten to detoxify the

Slightly sweet and nutty, peeled water chestnuts are perfect for snacking on fresh.

avoid invasive *trapa natans*

Beware: *Trapa natans*, also called water chestnut, is not the edible Chinese corm eaten as a vegetable. This water chestnut is an invasive aquatic plant that chokes out native aquatic plants along streams and lakes in the northeastern part of the United States. This annual plant appears as a rosette of small fan-shaped leaves that sit on the surface of the water. Underneath, air bladders near the top of long stems help keep the plant afloat. In late summer, the invasive plant produces seeds with four sharp spines on them that somewhat resemble *Eleocharis dulcis*. These seeds sink to the bottom of the body of water where they can remain dormant for over a decade until they sprout. Canadian geese may also carry the seeds to different locations.

body, help cure jaundice, and relieve coughs. Water chestnuts are high in fiber, vitamin B6, and potassium. They also contain trace amounts of many other minerals as well as epicatechin, the same powerful antioxidant found in green tea and red wine.

IN THE GARDEN In China, water chestnuts are typically grown in rotation with rice in the wet fields. Although corms are planted in early spring, it takes 6–8 months for a sizable corm to form, so water chestnuts are often thought of as a fall harvest. Those with full sun, a long hot season, and a pond or bog can try planting corms directly at the water's edge in light sandy soil. Fresh water chestnuts purchased at an Asian supermarket will taste delicious but often won't sprout. It's best to buy water chestnut corms from a source that sells them specifically for planting.

In zones 7 and higher, plant the corms about 4 inches deep and 18 inches apart in early spring. The water level should always be about 2 inches above the soil line. Water chestnuts are not an aquatic plant, but they do need a wet, mucky environment to grow. Creating an underwater shelf at the edge of the pond would produce great results.

Those of us with neither tropical climate nor natural water garden can still grow water chestnuts successfully. In zones 6 and below, sprout the corms indoors before the weather warms to help extend the season.

Fresh, crisp water chestnuts
taste like a cross between
a crisp apple and young
coconut.

Indoors in late winter, fill any container (buckets, storage bins, small tubs, shallow plastic wading pools) to 2–3 inches from the top with a rich, sandy soil. Plant corms about 4 inches deep and keep soil damp. When the corms sprout their reed-like hollow leaves and grow to 8 inches tall, bring the container outside after any chance of frost has passed. Fill with water to cover the soil line by about 2 inches. Remember to keep the water level consistent throughout the season.

When the leaves die back in the fall, carefully dig the corms from the pond's edge or drain the water from the container. Gently rinse off any mud. Be sure to save some of the largest corms to replant next season. Water chestnut plants cannot survive the hard freeze of a cold Northern winter. To save corms for replanting, bury them in damp soil or sand and store in a cool, dark place. Be sure they don't dry out during storage. Gardeners in frost-free climates can replant immediately.

IN THE KITCHEN Water chestnuts are slightly sweet, making them great in both desserts and savory dishes. To prepare fresh water chestnuts, pare the thin papery brown skin and cut into chunks or slices to use. Add water chestnuts to any dish in which you would enjoy the crisp, crunchy texture—typically stir-fries, dumplings, egg rolls, fresh salads, coconut drinks, and sweet desserts. Water chestnuts do not need to be cooked; simply add them to the dish near the end of the cooking time to heat through. In my kitchen, the best way to enjoy water chestnuts is as a snack; freshly pared and cut into slices like a miniature, crisp apple.

Benincasa hispida

winter melon

冬瓜

MANDARIN *dōngguā*
CANTONESE *dong gwaa*

Gardeners and cooks alike love winter melon's great taste, formidable size, and months-long storage ability—even up to a year under ideal conditions. These large, heavy gourds are related to fuzzy melon and have a similar pleasant taste. When immature, winter melons are often covered in soft downy hairs; as they mature, their downy hairs are replaced by a waxy coating, resulting in an ashy appearance (hence other common names wax gourd and ash gourd).

Winter melon is not sweet, and in fact, has little taste on its own. It is a vegetable that takes on the flavor of whatever it is cooked with. Because of its very

Winter melon develops a waxy coating as it matures, earning its common name wax gourd.

high water content, winter melon is the quintessential soup ingredient. A bowl of winter melon soup is a comforting and nourishing meal. It is light and easy to digest, acts as a good general tonic for the body, and has a cooling and calming effect, according to Chinese medicine. The gourd is also low in calories, high in dietary fiber, and known for supplying high doses of vitamin C.

Winter melon is not just for the convalescing, but is also an elegant food. The velvety texture and mild juicy flesh of the winter melon glistens in beautiful translucency when simmered in large chunks in simple soups. In the hands of a skilled and artistic chef, the large gourds can also be elaborately carved in bas-relief fashion (often with auspicious symbols or motifs) and turned into a natural soup tureen. In this case, the soup-filled melon is steamed whole for hours and is a showstopper when brought to the table. To serve, the flavorful soup is ladled out along with a chunk of tender melon.

IN THE GARDEN Winter melon needs warm soil and long hot days to produce large fruit. They do well in most climates of North America, but in colder climates with shorter growing seasons it may be a good idea to start plants indoors in order to get a head start or look for smaller varieties, which usually require fewer days to maturity.

In mid-spring after soil begins to dry out and warm up, prepare soil in a well-draining area of the garden by building mounds a few inches high, about 12 inches in diameter, and with a raised lip around the edge to help catch and retain water. Space mounds about 8 feet apart to give vigorous vines room to grow. Most varieties of winter melon contain seeds with very hard seed coats; soak seeds in water for a day or so before planting one or two seeds an inch deep in each mound. Keep soil well-watered, supplementing if there is little rain.

Allowing plants to ramble across the garden is the best way to grow large and healthy winter melons. Seeds are available for smaller varieties of gourds, which may be trained to grow up a strong trellis. Once established, winter melon grows into big plants with thick stems and sturdy leaves. My father's heirloom

Winter melon vines require room to grow—full-sized melons can weigh more than 40 pounds.

dong gwaa ramble over a large area in his garden. By fall, the slightly oblong gourds are gigantic and can weigh more than 40 pounds.

Harvest plants for fresh eating at any stage. When the gourds are small, green, and immature, they taste sweeter. As the gourds mature, the taste becomes blander and they develop their distinctive wax-covered look. This wax offers a protective layer, helping to extend the shelf life of the winter melon to many months. At the end of the season, harvest any remaining winter melons and store in a shed, cellar, or other cool, dry area.

IN THE KITCHEN By far the most common use for winter melon is in some version of a classic light soup. Strongly flavored ingredients (such as black mushroom, dried shrimp or scallops, cured ham, chicken, pork, ginger, goji berries, or dried red dates) complement the mild flavor of the gourd. There are primarily two methods of cooking winter melon. One method involves simmering large, pure white chunks of the melon in soup until they become translucent and tender. The other method is to shred the juicy flesh of the melon to produce a soup with a thicker and more pureed consistency. Either method results in a soup that is light in taste, juicy and flavorful, and perfect on its own or for accompanying a meal.

Prepare the winter melon for cooking by cutting into wedges of manageable size. Scoop away the seeds, cut the flesh from the hard rind, and slice into chunks or wedges. Wrap and refrigerate any pieces that you are not going to use right away. Once cut, winter melon should be used within a week.

In China and other parts of Southeast Asia, winter melon punch is a popular end-of-summer drink made by cooking down winter melon pieces with water and sugar until a sweet brown punch remains. It's then strained and chilled into a cooling, refreshing beverage. Some people also juice the winter melon raw, which produces a drink touted to help cure stomach ulcers when taken on an empty stomach in the morning. Candied or pureed winter melon pieces are also used as a filling in popular Chinese desserts such as moon cakes, or wife cakes, a flaky flat pastry.

TRADITIONAL WINTER MELON SOUP

Winter melon is almost always eaten in soup. The juiciness of the flesh—mild with a hint of sweet—complements the strongly flavored ingredients such as dried shiitake mushrooms, ham, and seafood. It is excellent on a cold winter's day. This traditional soup is easy to make but a couple of the dried ingredients do require some rehydrating time, so plan accordingly.

SERVES 4–6

1½ pounds winter melon (a long wedge or two of a large melon)

6 dried shrimp, soaked in water until soft, about 4 hours

5 dried shiitake mushrooms, soaked in water until soft, about 1 hour

2 tablespoons corn or peanut oil

3 green onions, cut into 2-inch lengths

6 slices of ginger, about ¼ inch thick

6 cups chicken stock

¼ pound cured ham, julienned

4 tablespoons cornstarch stirred into ⅓ cup water

Salt and white pepper

1 teaspoon dark (toasted) sesame oil

Several cilantro sprigs, chopped for garnish

1. Remove the seeds and cut the rind away from the winter melon. Cut the melon into generous bite-sized chunks. Drain the dried shrimp and shiitake mushrooms. Cut any corky stems off the mushrooms and cut them into ⅓-inch-wide slices.

2. Add the oil to a large pot over high heat. When hot, add the dried shrimp, onions, and ginger, and stir-fry until fragrant, 1 or 2 minutes. Add the winter melon, chicken stock, mushrooms, and ham. Bring to a boil, and then reduce heat to simmer for about 25 minutes. When ready, the winter melon pieces should be translucent and cooked to a velvety texture.

3. Add the cornstarch solution to the soup to thicken slightly. Cook for a few more minutes and season with salt and pepper to taste. Drizzle the sesame oil into the soup and remove from the heat. To serve, garnish with cilantro.

WINTER

Every now and then, I ask my father questions about his garden in China, knowing that this is the vehicle for learning more about his childhood life. Asking about the vegetables he grew and how he grew them gives him a safe route to tell me about a life from the distant past that was as tough as it was bucolic.

The climate in my father's Shandong, China, is much like our climate in the Mid-Atlantic region of the United States. We have similar hot summers, cold winters with hard freezes and snow storms, and beautiful spring and fall seasons. Even the clay soil is similar. It was easy for him to take his gardening ▶

My father loves tatsoi, especially after it has become sweetened by frost.

experience and pick up where he left off after arriving in America in the mid-1970s. Fortunately, what he did not have to carry over was the necessity of growing vegetables as the sole source of food.

In early winter before the ground froze solid, my father, my uncle, and my grandmother dug large pits several feet wide and deep in their nearby garden. Then, if they were lucky, they would be able to borrow a wheelbarrow or wagon for the walk further out to the family's larger growing fields. They would harvest cold-weather crops such as Napa cabbages, radishes, and winter squash and bring them back to the pits in the garden. There, they were buried for use throughout the winter. As he told the story, I loved the image of the Napa cabbages upside down, neatly lined up and stacked several levels high. When the cabbages neared the soil line, they would be covered with dirt, leaves, and later snow and stored until they were needed. The cabbages would be buried upside down with roots facing up to prevent the inner leaves from being covered in loose dirt. The upward-facing roots also provided an easy way to fish for and grab the hefty heads of cabbage. During the coldest days of winter, my father would go out to the pit and dig out two or three heads of cabbage to last his family the week. Several large and beautiful cabbages would also be buried in the pit, but stacked right-side up with roots facing down. This was my family's way to designate the seed cabbages that would be transplanted into the garden in the spring. When summer approached, the cabbages would flower and their seeds would be saved for fall planting.

I grew up not knowing the hunger and the hard work required to stave off that hunger that my relatives just one generation back experienced. I'm saddened that this was a life my father and his family lived, but I am also empowered by their ingenuity. With handfuls of seed along with intellect, determination, and physical work, they created everything they needed to survive throughout the year, including the harsh winter months, in a place where refrigerators, grocery stores, and even basic living conveniences such as heat and plumbing were nonexistent. These stories keep me inspired to learn more about growing and preserving my own food. When I harvest herbs, greens, or radishes from under snow cover in my own garden, I feel a small spark of connection with the boy my father was, and the grandmother I never knew.

the winter garden and growing in cold frames

The winter garden can be a vibrant landscape of food. While it takes some effort to keep things going in my zone 6 garden, gardeners in zones more northern than mine regularly and successfully grow a rainbow of foods in lush gardens covered in several feet of snow. When I think of winter gardening, the first thing that often comes to mind is a cold frame, which is basically a bottomless box with a translucent top that captures solar energy. I cannot pass by someone's scrapped window next to the trash without grand thoughts of dragging it home to craft a cold frame. My ancestors in China used an almost identical version—what they called solar frames—to keep harvests going through the winter season. Clearly gardeners on both sides of the globe considered cold-season gardening needs and fashioned the same simple box for growing vegetables that would keep out harsh winds, freezing rain, and snow, let sunlight in, and create a microclimate in which plants can thrive throughout the winter.

To build a cold frame, simply provide four walls and a clear or translucent cover. You can build the walls from rot-resistant wood, brick, cinderblocks, or straw bales. Angle the side walls so that they are taller in the back of the frame and shorter in the front. When facing south, this allows for maximum light to be captured. The slope also allows rain and snow to roll off. For the cover of the frame, often called the light, you can use an old framed window, shower door, or a heavy polycarbonate material that allows light to pass through. In China, most gardeners sink their cold frames several inches into the ground, providing further insulation for the vegetables.

A cold frame can be a permanent structure such as a wooden box with its cover on hinges that can be adjusted to allow air circulation in the box. It can

Cold frames allow gardeners to plant early and then extend the harvesting season through the coldest days of winter.

Remember to vent the cold frame on mild winter days when the microclimate inside the cold frame may get too warm.

also be as temporary as setting four straw bales in your garden and covering them with a heavy sheet of plastic, fastened into the dirt with rocks. In China, many neat and temporary solar frames are constructed directly in the fields in late fall in preparation for the winter. Called solar beds or winter beds, these are made by digging down to build a sunken bed facing south and piling up the soil along the back side to construct one of the walls. Bamboo poles are then placed on top to support the glass or plastic covers. If more protection is needed, straw, leaves, or other light but insulating materials could be added on top of the cover.

The concept and construction of the cold frame is relatively simple, but it takes more thought to figure out the timing for growing vegetables in it. In my zone, I begin seeding most cold-hardy vegetables (such as radishes, Chinese cabbages, and stem lettuce) in late summer to early fall. At this point, I can plant them in the cold frame without needing the cover. I sow quick-growing lettuces a month later. Many weeks later, as frost approaches, I add the cover to protect the plants from damage. While growth slows as we enter the winter season, the plants continue to be fresh and alive, later even frost-sweetened, and ready for harvest when you need them.

As you harvest vegetables and spots in the cold frame open up, you can sow new cold-hardy plants. When sowing seeds during the height of winter, germination rates can be dicey. Although some seeds may germinate, some may sit patiently in the ground until early spring, and some may rot. Soil temperature, seasonal temperature fluctuations, rain levels, and my troublesome dogs are all factors that determine whether new crops may grow. Some seasons I have better luck than others but for me, it is always worth the cost of the seeds to try. Alternatively, you may wait until late winter when days begin to lengthen, temperatures become milder, and the cold frame is nearly empty and ready for sowing again. At this time, you can start cold-tolerant vegetables such as bok choy, gailan, and chrysanthemum greens. Because the top of a cold frame needs to be lowered in harsh weather, I try to stay away from plants that can get too tall too fast such as peas. However, you can certainly grow snow peas in the cold frame for the purpose of harvesting their tender shoots in the early spring before they get too tall.

Gardeners like me who look forward to a quiet respite from actively gardening for a season have all the benefits of harvesting vegetables whenever we want, while knowing the real work was done months ago. Growing winter vegetables requires practically no work. The most important consideration is venting the cold frame so plants don't cook. While the purpose of using a cold frame is to create a protected microclimate in which vegetables can thrive, the environment can quickly and suddenly get too warm and too humid. In the mild early winter, or during the thaw of late winter to early spring, daytime temperatures can be balmy. As a general guideline, when outdoor temperatures reach 40 degrees Fahrenheit, use a stick to prop the lid open a few inches to ventilate the cold frame. If outdoor temperatures reach 50 degrees Fahrenheit outdoors, open the cover all the way. Just don't forget to put the cover back on before it gets cold that evening.

Winter gardeners can even take a lackadaisical approach to watering, the most basic and incessant gardening chore. During most of the winter, evaporation slows greatly and plants rarely need water. However, on either end of the season, temperatures in the cold frame may be warm enough that plants need to be watered. Water only when the soil is completely dry, and do it during the warmest part of the day, focusing on the root zone and not the leaves.

more on winter protection

Cold frames aren't the only way to keep fall vegetables growing into the winter or to start cold-hardy vegetables that grow into the spring. Other methods range from using cloche-like covers (which you can recycle from materials such as clean milk jugs with the bottoms cut off or old inverted fish tanks) to growing in traditional greenhouses. For the temporary protection of individual plants, gardeners in China used clay pots to cover and protect plants from wind, heavy rain, or light frosts. My father used this method when growing cilantro in 1950s Shandong, China. Before the first freeze, he would dig a few cilantro plants out of the garden, roots and all, and transplant them to a patch of dirt in the open-aired, dirt-floored courtyard in the center of the family's home. He would cover the cilantro with a pot and then cover the pot with dried corn stalks. The clay pot kept the soil moist and protected the cilantro from killing freezes so it could continue growing. With this method, cilantro remained available for fresh use for 2–3 months until early spring, at which point he could sow new crops in the garden. Sometimes upon uncovering the cilantro the leaves would be frost-covered, but still green and just short of frozen.

In the earliest days of winter, I sometimes use floating row covers to extend the season. This airy cloth sits right on top of my vegetables, letting in moisture and light while providing some minimal protection against dropping temperatures. I also use this same lightweight cover during the summer months to protect against certain pests in the garden. These thin row covers provide a slightly warmer environment, but won't protect plants from frost. Heavier weight row covers, sometimes called frost blankets, transmit less light so they are best used as temporary covers. They may be a good idea for gardeners in warmer climates that face intermittent threats of frost.

A hoop house is another structure that provides winter protection. It basically consists of a large sheet of plastic film stretched over supports made from PVC or metal conduit hoops. Hoop houses shelter vegetables from the elements just like cold frames, but are effective with a larger planting area. A hoop house that is large enough to walk through is sometimes known as a high tunnel. A low tunnel, on the other hand, looks similar to my row of vegetables under the floating row cover, except that it is built with the addition of small hoops underneath that hold up a heavier weight plastic sheet several inches above—not touching—the plants. Gardeners can also try doubling up the protection by growing a row of plants under a low tunnel that is inside a high tunnel. In China, some of these structures, known as hothouses, are enhanced with heaters or lamps that provide heat as well.

To provide even more protection and warmth, situate any of the previously mentioned structures so that plants are facing south, but against a windbreak, which may be the side of the house, a wall, a fence, or row of shrubs. Placing straw bales around the garden, or at least on the north side where the harshest winter winds come from, may also offer some protection during winter.

frost-sweetened vegetables

Like all living things, plants contain water. When frozen, the cells of tender plants expand and then burst, causing the plants to wilt or turn to mush. However, certain vegetables like tatsoi and daikon radishes (and Western vegetables such as carrots and kale) actually taste better after they're hit with a few hard frosts. In response to very cold temperatures, these frost-tolerant plants convert some of their starches to sugar. Increased sugar helps to keep the plants' cells from freezing and becoming frost-damaged, similar to how applying salt to roads keeps water from freezing on the surface. This protective process also happens to make vegetables taste noticeably sweeter.

It is also crucial to mulch plants before it gets too cold. Organic materials such as shredded leaves, straw, or shredded hardwood bark all work well. While summer mulching is about keeping weeds down and preserving moisture, the main purpose of winter mulching is to provide some insulation for plants. About 2 inches of mulch is sufficient.

My friend Josh, community garden specialist at D.C. Department of Parks and Recreation, uses water bottles to warm up the winter garden. To try his cheap trick, paint recycled milk jugs black and fill them with water and salt to create a saturated salt solution. Black absorbs heat from sunlight and the salt water helps the jugs retain heat. Place these jugs facing south and among your plants in the garden, hoop house, or cold frame: the heat captured during the day will help keep plants warmer at night.

hardy and delicious winter vegetables

With a little protection from the elements, many vegetables will continue growing right through the coldest, snowiest days of winter. Under row covers or cold frames in the Chinese vegetable garden you may find hearty leafy greens (such as tatsoi and other cabbages), mustards, peas, turnips, kohlrabi, beets, and herbs (like chives or cilantro). A coating of frost on these frost-tolerant plants is usually not a problem. Leafy greens in particular may look wilted sometimes, but they will bounce back in warmer temperatures. Because the sun is lower in the sky and days are shorter, winter vegetables may not appear to be actively growing during the winter, but they are certainly alive and will be ready for harvest whenever you want them.

Some root vegetables such as radishes can remain in the ground where they've been growing. They will often overwinter just fine, especially with a little protection in colder zones such as a layer of straw or a row cover. Keep the garden weeded so weeds aren't overwintering along with the vegetables. The leafy tops may die off so it's a good idea to mark where each root is located under the soil line so you know where to dig when the time comes.

Just as most summer vegetables are best harvested in the cooler early morning hours, winter vegetables are best when harvested during the warmest part of the afternoon. This is when the sun warms the interior of the cold frame or hoop house enough to defrost the vegetables. If you harvest frozen vegetables from the garden, you may end up with a basketful of mush once they have defrosted on your kitchen counter. So be sure to pay attention to when you harvest for the best taste and texture—after all, you didn't keep the faith all winter to have less-than-perfect vegetables.

cleaning up and winterizing

Part of my annual garden clean up involves preparing for frozen weather which can wreck tools and accessories in my garden. Just before it gets too cold to work outside, I gather leftover items from the garden to store in the shed. This includes bamboo stakes, tomato cages, moveable trellises, any hand tools left in the garden, and anything made of plastic that may crack in harsh weather. I give my tools—which have been faithfully cutting, digging, moving, and trimming for months—a proper cleaning before storing them for winter.

I'm always careful with small items that could become covered in leaves. Come spring, I would not like my lawn mower to find these things before I do. Similarly, I don't want to stumble upon any sharp objects left out and hidden by new spring growth. I drain and cover my rain barrel and set the water diverter to flow away from the house. While I always think I will remember exactly how many good pea fences I have, or how many bags of mulch I have left in the shed, this is a good time to take inventory. This way, I am free to sit indoors and plan during the winter season without needing to bundle up, run to the shed, and check if I have enough pots to start seeds in early spring.

planning and organizing

While I'm often envious of my friends who live in tropical zones and can grow all kinds of fantastic flowers, fruits, and vegetables year round, the reality is, this gardener gets tired. I count on the winter season to rest and reset. I need this time to regain confidence, and I depend on what I call winter amnesia to forget the aphids that destroyed my lettuce, the flea beetles that shot my eggplants with pinholes, the blight that took many fruits, and the week I took a trip and my garden suffered a drought. This period of rest recharges me and allows me to reflect on what happened so I can set some new resolutions. As much as I love my garden, I need a little bit of away time to make the next year even better.

Away time doesn't mean I'm not still every bit as obsessed as I usually am about gardening. It just means I'm inside thinking about gardening instead of digging in the dirt. I look at my notes from earlier in the year, make adjustments to next year's seed sowing dates, remind myself about things that went wrong (such as starting fall vegetables too late), and reminisce on things that went right like (loosely) emulating Thomas Jefferson's method of sowing a thimbleful of seed every Monday to keep greens growing for a very long season. Actually, I always end up thanking myself at some point for practicing another Thomas Jeffersonism: keeping meticulous notes. This is the only sure way I remember how many bales of straw I need to keep my vegetables mulched all season, my family's favorite varieties of heirloom peppers, and my father's method for building a trellis out of bamboo. Without keeping a good garden journal, it's just too easy to forget.

All summer, I open and use seed packets, and then just toss them back into a basket of gardening junk. Now is my time for organization. Each winter, I make a list of every vegetable I would like to grow and make sure I have seeds for those vegetables. If not, I make a point to place my seed order before seed-starting time begins in late winter or early spring. When I have all my seeds in front of me, I separate each seed packet or jar into piles according to how and when I will start them. I create separate piles for vegetables with long growing seasons that are to be started indoors, cold-tolerant plants to sow outdoors in early spring, tender plants to start after danger of frost has passed, summer vegetables to sow when the soil has warmed, and finally, a fall vegetable seeds pile.

Like many gardeners, I'm a seed hoarder. I invariably end up with seeds that are many years old, but that I don't have the heart to throw away. This can be a problem because seeds, while dormant, are living things and over time their germination rates decrease. Using old seeds with poor germination can be a waste of time and energy. It is disappointing when weeks of loving care of little pots go by and a sprout never emerges. It can also delay your harvest time.

When faced with a large amount of older seeds for a certain vegetable, I do this simple germination test to determine their viability before planting in spring. Place about twenty seeds on a wet (not dripping) paper towel, fold the paper towel in half, and put it in a plastic bag. Position the bag in a suitable environment for the particular type of seed, information that is often listed on the seed packet. For example, peppers benefit from warmth during germination. After a few days, remove the paper towel and count how many seeds germinated. Remove those sprouts, dampen the paper towel and leave for another day or two before checking again. Lettuces are quick to germinate whereas seeds like bitter melon are notoriously slow. When you're pretty certain no further seeds will germinate (use the days-to-germination information on the seed packet as a guide), count the number of seeds that have sprouted. If most of the seeds germinated, they are perfectly viable. If 50 percent germinated, you may consider sowing twice the amount you normally would. Seeds that have a lower germination rate and are germinating more slowly than typical may not be worth planting. It will be less frustrating to simply start from scratch with fresh seeds.

expanding the garden

The one activity I'm sure to engage in every year is trying to find a way to increase the area of my garden. Unlucky gardeners like me have lots of issues to work around: tall trees that cast shade over certain spots in my yard, large tree roots that make in-ground gardening difficult, and little persistent beagles that like to sniff, dig, and climb garden fences.

One thing I've done to address the shade issue is to pick a day and chart where the sun hits my garden by checking every hour. This exercise helps me map out sunny areas from which I can squeeze more gardening space. I do keep in mind that the winter sun is going to track differently than the summer sun, but I can get a general sense of areas in my yard that will likely get the eight plus

Support structures like trellises allow tall bitter melon to climb, making use of vertical space and leaving room on the ground for more plants.

hours required for most of my sun-loving fruiting vegetables like bitter melon and gourds, and the areas that get less sun where I might plant my herbs and lettuces that tolerate more shade.

The blank canvas of a winter garden makes it possible to really evaluate your space and envision new possibilities. During one particular winter when I could find no more space to expand my raised beds, I looked out at a mostly empty landscape and realized I could grow more vegetables by going vertical with trellises. Another year, when my garden met a good balance of row space and climbing space, I realized I could add large pots and planters to unused spots on the patio. And one winter when I saw that all the prime ground space had been utilized, I looked for places here and there where plants could be tucked in, like in containers among ornamentals, in unused window boxes where flowers usually grow, or in my perennial gardens. Because the winter garden is bare and you see just the bones of the garden, this is a particularly good time of year to visualize new gardens. If I attempt the same sort of visualization during the summer, I'm too distracted by the weeds to be pulled, the shrubs to be pruned, and the vegetables to be harvested.

sprouting

When I'm looking for a way to get something fresh and healthful into my diet during the bleakest days of winter, I start a batch of sprouts. My ancestors have been prescribing sprouts as medicine for more than five thousand years. Though no one is exactly sure how those dosages were carried out, I do know that sprouts have a way of jolting your body into a feeling of vitality. Sprouts are loaded with nutrition. The sprouts of all vegetables generally have the same or a much higher nutritional value than what was present in the seed. Sprouted mung beans and sprouted soybeans have a greater amount of amino acids than their whole bean forms after dark protein is broken down into amino acids during the germination process. Bean sprouts have also been found to effectively regulate blood sugar. They are high in B-complex vitamins and vitamins A and C, and the amount of protein in sprouted mung beans increases exponentially after sprouting.

Many beans besides well-known mung beans make excellent sprouts. These include soybeans and red beans (which produce a larger sprout than mung beans), mustard greens and other Chinese brassicas, chrysanthemum greens, peas, radishes, and onions. Each of these seeds produces a sprout unique in appearance, texture, and taste. Mustards, for example, produce thin, hot sprouts, whereas broccoli produces crisp, mild sprouts. You can use sprouts in many different ways, from sandwich ingredients to side salads. Once you've tried sprouting a few different kinds of seeds, you can even experiment by creating a variety of seed combinations. I've sprouted a spicy mix of different types of mustards and radishes that looked delicate but offered a strong, delicious bite.

To grow a quick container of nutritious sprouts all you need are a few spoonfuls of seed (make certain they have not been chemically treated) and a container for starting the sprouts. I use a container that has an insert with a sieve-like bottom; this allows water to drain into an outside container that catches any water drips. Other containers like large canning jars, recycled food containers, and large carry-out soup containers all work. A DIY sprouter is easy to make and the Internet offers many ideas. The container just needs to be large enough to allow the seeds to sprout and grow to ten times their original size.

Before you begin, be sure that all your sprouting materials are very clean. To produce a final product of about 3 cups of loose sprouts, use about

Growing bean sprouts is a
tasty and easy food project
perfect for cold winter days.

sprout safety

Sprouted legumes can contain toxins when eaten raw. It is fine to eat raw sprouted beans and peas in small amounts, but if you use them regularly and in large amounts, it is a good idea to cook them first by steaming, boiling, or stir-frying. Sprouts may also put one at risk of getting sick due to bacteria that was present in the seed and because the process of sprouting requires a damp, crowded, warm environment, which is also conducive to multiplying bacteria. I minimize risks by keeping my sprouting materials extremely clean and by rinsing the seeds three times a day.

2 tablespoons of seeds. A more accurate measure of the amount of seeds needed depends on the type of seed you are sprouting, but a little more or a little less won't affect your sprouting. On day one, soak seeds for 8–12 hours in three times as much water. After the initial soaking, drain well. The following step will be the same for the next few days: every 8 hours or so, rinse the seeds in cool water, drain well, and loosely cover. Place the sprouting container where it won't be disturbed and where you will remember to rinse and drain them. My sprouting container sits in a quiet area on my kitchen counter. Repeat the rinsing and draining process three times a day, every day for the next 5 days or so.

When the cotyledons begin to open up and the hulls of the seeds are starting to come off easily, the sprouts are nearly done. At this point, remove the cover and move the container to a sunnier spot if you want. Within just a few hours, the tiny baby plants will begin to green up. Green sprouts are generally more nutritious, while white sprouts that are deprived of light tend to be crisper, a texture some people prefer. Mung beans are generally deprived of light to maintain their light color and juicy crunch.

When the sprouts are ready, rinse them one last time by swishing around in a big bowl of water. Scoop out any seed hulls that float to the top of the water and add them to the compost. Fresh sprouts deteriorate nearly as quickly as they germinate so store sprouts in the refrigerator and use within a few days.

Most delicate sprouts like alfalfa are eaten raw, and the more substantial mung bean sprouts can be eaten raw too, such as in a spring roll or to top a bowl

Mung bean seeds on day two of sprouting. They will be ready in just a few more days.

of Vietnamese pho or Japanese ramen noodles. In Chinese cuisine, mung bean sprouts are often steamed or stir-fried. One of my favorite dishes is a stir-fry of wide flat rice noodles with sliced beef, onions, and bean sprouts. This dish can't be beat, especially when it's from a restaurant kitchen's sizzling wok over a high, hot flame.

microgreens

Growing your own microgreens is another convenient way to add a nutritional superfood to your diet during the winter season. While sprouts are the germinated or sprouted seeds of vegetables, microgreens are tiny plants, even younger than plants in the baby leaf stage. When my garden is still covered in snow but I'm eager to play around with seeds and soil, I start a tray of microgreens. Coincidentally, the timing of this activity usually matches right up with New Year's resolutions to eat more healthily.

Because of their delicate baby leaves and ultra-thin stems, microgreens are often served atop elegant foods, but they should not be mistaken for a simple garnish. While these greens appear tiny, they hold a flavor that is true. Mustard microgreens, consisting of two perfect "first" leaves and a threadlike stem, have a hot flavor like they have in the mature stage. Microgreens are widely regarded as nutritionally superior as well. Studies have found that a wide variety of microgreens contain four to forty times more vitamins C, E, and K, beta-carotene, and other nutrients than their mature counterparts.

You can grow many vegetables to be eaten as microgreens. I love an attractive mix of greens brightened with micro-vegetables of other colors such as reds and purples. Some great choices of Chinese vegetables to grow as microgreens include daikon and green radishes, peas, amaranth, cilantro, garland chrysan-themum, mustards, and other leaf lettuces. To help preserve their nutritional value, always eat them raw—just quickly rinse if necessary.

Growing a fresh batch of microgreens is practically foolproof, and is a particularly good project to do with children of any age. My younger child can complete all the tasks from beginning to end with no supervision. I can typically find several suitable containers for planting in my recycling bin. Containers should be wide but only need to be a few inches deep. After cleaning these containers, I cut holes through the bottom for drainage. Potting soil, seeds, and a spray bottle are the only other materials needed.

To grow microgreens, fill clean containers with a few inches of potting soil and sow seeds thickly, with little to no space in between. You will be harvesting plants shortly after germination so you don't need to worry about giving each seedling room to grow. Gently press seeds into soil and then sprinkle a fine layer of soil over top. Spray gently with water, being careful not to disturb seeds, until all the soil in the container is moist. Situate the container in a sunny spot and spray with water daily to keep soil moist. Seeds should germinate within 3–5 days. Continue spraying with water and microgreens will be ready to harvest in 7–10 days when plants are about 2 inches high. You will be harvesting the cotyledons and the thin stems below. They are sometimes harvested with their first set of true leaves as well. The easiest way to harvest is to simply snip with scissors and gently rinse if necessary. Many leafy vegetables will actually regrow, and late-germinating seed may also have sent up sprouts that missed the first cutting, so continue to water the container after your first harvest. Use microgreens within a few days as they will wilt just as quickly as they grow.

Although microgreens are not a traditional part of Chinese cuisine, Chinese vegetables make excellent microgreens and are a potent garnish to enhance the flavor in both Asian and Western dishes. Finish hors d'oeuvres with a sprinkling of delicate thin-stemmed microgreens or drop them on top of an open-faced sandwich. Microgreens add great texture, visual interest, and flavor to just about any food. In my house, we like to enjoy freshly harvested microgreens as a salad with a little bit of a light dressing.

For many gardeners, winter is a well-needed time of rest and reflection.

taking a well-deserved break

While small food-growing projects happen periodically in the winter, I'm grateful for a short period when garden work slows and I can do all the things I was not able to do during the rest of the year. I usually collect some books and magazines and have marathon reading sessions since I have more free time inside. No matter how many years you've been gardening, there are always new ideas to try and old ones to revisit. This is a time for learning about different varieties of vegetables you haven't grown before and for making garden resolutions.

For me, winter is a time to write, reflect, and talk to gardeners, especially seasoned ones like my father who hold decades of stories and experience. When talking to my father, I learn about old world gardening, like how he would strip young flexible twigs from mulberry trees to create a super strong and pliable material for tying off the top of a bamboo trellis. Surely my father would think it was silly that I was stripping mulberry twigs instead of purchasing twine from the store. But learning and then practicing these old methods feels like a connection to my culture and to people and a world I never got to know. I also love to research and practice skills of self-sufficiency such as food preservation. I believe it ties me to all the gardeners before me, much like a collective "om" during yoga connects one to all the other practitioners in the world.

The truth is, of all the seasons, winter is my favorite. The season has so much beauty in its quietude that my husband and I named our first child Winter.

good luck in the new year

Chinese vegetables play a large, enchanting role in symbolic meals and traditions, especially around the Lunar New Year, which always falls near the end of winter and is the biggest celebration in Hong Kong, China, and much of Asia. Plants that symbolize fortune, such as kumquats (*gum* in Cantonese, a homophone for gold), are given as gifts or used to decorate the house. My parents make a big dinner full of symbolic foods, such as a fish (*yue* in Cantonese, a homophone for abundance). My father's dumplings are particularly special as he hides coins in a few, bringing good luck in the upcoming year to whoever finds them. My favorite tradition is the Chinese lion dance—a beautiful and colorful martial art form with bright, ornate costumes and drumming so intense you can feel it in your heart. The performance culminates with someone feeding the lion a real head of cabbage (*choy* in Cantonese, a homophone for fortune). A long dramatic pause follows, punctuated by a soft clattering of the gongs, during which the lion is chewing. Then the cymbals clash loudly and the drums resume beating as the lion spits out the shredded cabbage, showering fortune on the people.

When I think about my intention during the time we chose to use this season as a name, I feel the brisk air on my face, and see a stark landscape of snow-covered trees, still streams, and solid ground. It is simplicity, peace, and calm.

However, if you don't share my opinions about winter and are counting the days until spring, consider the traditional folk wisdom of farmers in China to know when the willow trees will once again bud with leaves, the ground will soften, and you can go out and dig. As the general rule goes, following the first day of winter, there are two sets of 9 days, progressively getting colder. Then, there are two sets of 9 days that will be the coldest of the year. Two more sets of 9 days will get progressively warmer, and then spring will be right around the corner again.

metric conversions and plant hardiness zones

length

inches	cm		feet	m
¼	0.6		1	0.3
½	1.3		2	0.6
1	2.5		3	0.9
2	5.1		4	1.2
3	7.6		5	1.5
4	10		6	1.8
5	13		7	2.1
6	15		8	2.4
7	18		9	2.7
8	20		10	3
9	23		20	6
10	25		30	9
20	51		40	12
30	76		50	15
40	100		100	30
50	130			

weight

pounds	ounces	grams
¼	4	115
½	8	225
¾	12	340
1	16	454

temperatures

$$°C = \tfrac{5}{9} \times (°F-32)$$
$$°F = (\tfrac{9}{5} \times °C) + 32$$

plant hardiness zones

Average annual minimum temperature

zone	temperature (deg. F)	temperature (deg. C)
1	Below −50	Below −46
2	−50 to −40	−46 to −40
3	−40 to −30	−40 to −34
4	−30 to −20	−34 to −29
5	−20 to −10	−29 to −23
6	−10 to 0	−23 to −18
7	0 to 10	−18 to −12
8	10 to 20	−12 to −7
9	20 to 30	−7 to −1
10	30 to 40	−1 to 4
11	40 and above	4 and above

To see the U.S. Department of Agriculture Hardiness Zone Map, go to
http://planthardiness.ars.usda.gov/PHZMWeb/

resources and seed suppliers

This section lists some helpful online gardening resources and sources for quality seeds. I also recommend attending local seed swap events (visit seedswapday.com to learn more) and checking out the seeds available at your local Asian or international market.

resources

agnr.umd.edu/news/mighty-microgreens
almanac.com
bamboogarden.com
greenishthumb.net
groweat.blogspot.com
howtosaveseeds.com
motherearthnews.com
rodalesorganiclife.com
seedsavers.org
sproutpeople.org
vegetablegardener.com

seed suppliers

Baker Creek Heirloom Seeds
rareseeds.com

Botanical Interests
botanicalinterests.com

Evergreen Y.H. Enterprises
evergreenseeds.com

Johnny's Selected Seeds
johnnyseeds.com

Kitazawa Seed Company
kitazawaseed.com

Renee's Garden
reneesgarden.com

Seed Saver's Exchange
seedsavers.org

Southern Exposure Seed Exchange
southernexposure.com

recommended reading

Bradley, Fern Marshall, Barbara W. Ellis, and Ellen Phillips. *Rodale's Ultimate Encyclopedia of Organic Gardening*. New York, NY: Rodale, 2009.

Forkner, Lorene Edwards. *The Timber Press Guide to Vegetable Gardening in the Pacific Northwest*. Portland, OR: Timber Press, 2012.

Harrington, Geri. *Growing Chinese Vegetables in Your Own Backyard*. North Adams, MA: Storey Publishing, 2009.

Hutton, Wendy. *A Cook's Guide to Asian Vegetables*. North Clarendon, VT: Tuttle Publishing, 2004.

Iannotti, Marie. *The Beginner's Guide to Growing Heirloom Vegetables: The 100 Easiest-to Grow, Tastiest Vegetables for Your Garden*. Portland, OR: Timber Press, 2011.

Iannotti, Marie. *The Timber Press Guide to Vegetable Gardening in the Northeast*. Portland, OR: Timber Press, 2014.

Jabbour, Niki. *The Year Round Vegetable Gardener*. North Adams, MA: Storey Publishing, 2011.

Larkcom, Joy. *Oriental Vegetables: The Complete Guide for the Gardening Cook*. 2nd ed. New York, NY: Kodansha International, Ltd., 2008.

Lau, Anita Loh-Yien. *Asian Greens*. New York, NY: Quintet Publishing Limited, 2001.

Newcomer, Mary Ann. *The Timber Press Guide to Vegetable Gardening in the Mountain States*. Portland, OR: Timber Press, 2014.

Shirey, Trisha. *The Timber Press Guide to Vegetable Gardening in the Southwest*. Portland, OR: Timber Press, 2015.

Smetana, Jeanine, ed. *The University of Maryland Master Gardener Handbook*. Richmond, VA: University of Maryland Extension, 2008.

Tanumihardja, Pat. *The Asian Grandmother's Cookbook*. Seattle, WA: Sasquatch Books, 2012.

Wallace, Ira. *The Timber Press Guide to Vegetable Gardening in the Southeast*. Portland, OR: Timber Press, 2013.

Walliser, Jessica. *Attracting Beneficial Bugs to Your Garden: A Natural Approach to Pest Control*. Portland, OR: Timber Press, 2013.

Young, Grace, and Alan Richardson. *The Breath of a Wok*. New York, NY: Simon & Schuster, 2004.

acknowledgments

One of the luckiest days of my life was the day I crossed paths with Tom Fischer. Thank you Tom for believing in this book, for understanding exactly what I was trying to do with it, and for being excited and optimistic throughout this process. Through these pages about how deep to sow a seed or how long to stir-fry a vegetable, I was able to tell my family's story and we are eternally grateful for that opportunity.

Thank you Mollie Firestone for your mad grammar skills, meticulousness, and patience, and for helping me present my story to the world in the best shape possible. Thank you Eve Goodman for your kindness, encouragement, and management of this project. My sincere appreciation to Patrick Barber, Katlynn Nicolls, and all the good people at Timber Press I haven't named who have been a part of this project. Thank you for your energy and time.

Kudos to Sandy Farber Bandier, friend and UDC Extension Agent and Master Gardener Coordinator, for all you do for D.C. gardens and for providing opportunities to gardeners to learn and act on their passions for gardening.

Accolades to Kathy Jentz, editor and publisher of *Washington Gardener Magazine*, and facilitator of many, many activities for an immense community of gardeners and garden writers in our region.

Thanks to Niki Jabbour for being an inspiration to me and many gardeners around the world and for saying something to me once that directed the course of this ship.

I admire and am grateful for all the gardening friends I have made through social media from around the world who have read my work, spurred me on, inspired me with their own work, and shared in my excitement for growing beautiful and edible things.

Thanks to every workshop participant who has wanted to learn about Asian vegetables, and especially to those who have reached out and made a connection with me. I remember every comment from every new friend I've made. Thanks especially to the people in the past two years who have told me they cannot wait for this book to come out.

Thanks to my friend Samantha Morick who has never tired of asking me what's going on with the book. I'm so grateful to share life's ups, downs, and many milestones with you.

Thanks to my friend Jennifer Taylor, who has also never tired of asking me what's going on with the book, for being on this roller coaster with me, and for always making me think positively.

Thank you to Becky Warren, Joyce Ho, David Marciniak, and Ginger Mallard for being awesome recipe testers.

A sincere thank you to Carol Allen, Bruce Bailey, Grace Deitemyer, Lisa Kiang, and Erica Smith for your knowledge, questions, critical eye, ideas, encouragement, time, and support.

Thanks to my friend Grace Deitemyer who also never tires of asking what's going on with the book and for being my field trip buddy and partner in all things garden-related and beyond.

A huge thank you to the incredibly talented Sarah Culver, who can make anything a beautiful work of art, and who was able to create the images for this book that I only dreamed about in my head.

Thank you to my mother and father for sharing the stories with me. Thank you again for everything I've thanked you for in the past, and everything I have not yet put in words.

Thank you to my sister, Lisa Kiang, my eternal cheerleader and best friend in the world.

Thank you to my husband for patiently listening to and going along with every cockamamie idea I have ever had with never a shred of doubt. Well, except for the time I planned to rollerblade from Twinbrook to D.C., and as we both know, I made it. But besides that, you've always been right there with me, rooting me on.

Lisa and Skull, I don't think I'd be able to accomplish much of anything in life (let alone with this book) without your unwavering and unconditional love, enthusiasm, and confidence.

Thanks to Winter and Lyric for being kind, generous, and spectacularly interesting people, daughters who make life really easy and fun every single day, and for being loving and respectful granddaughters. Thank you Winter for asking if we could have a garden. Thank you Lyric for picking strawberries with me every June.

photo credits

Wendy Kiang-Spray, pages 18, 22, 24, 36, 56, 64, 83, 103 top, 136, 139 right, 144, 147 bottom, 148, 171, 189, 197 right, 198, 217, 221
Kiang family, page 5 center

All other photos are by Sarah Culver.

index

WENDY KIANG-SPRAY's articles about gardening and food have appeared in national, local, and web publications. She comes from a long line of gardeners passionate about growing food but is fortunate to be the first generation in her family not reliant upon farming for survival. When she's not working in her garden, she is a high school counselor, garden speaker, and volunteer with the DC Master Gardeners. Wendy blogs about gardening, food projects, and family at www.greenishthumb.net and about Asian vegetables at www.wendykiangspray.com.

Sarah Culver